Mobile Development with C#

Greg Shackles

O'REILLY®

Beijing · Cambridge · Farnham · Köln · Sebastopol · Tokyo

Mobile Development with C#
by Greg Shackles

Published by O'Reilly Media, Inc., 1005 Gravenstein Highway North, Sebastopol, CA 95472.

O'Reilly books may be purchased for educational, business, or sales promotional use. Online editions are also available for most titles (*http://my.safaribooksonline.com*). For more information, contact our corporate/institutional sales department: 800-998-9938 or *corporate@oreilly.com*.

Editor: Rachel Roumeliotis   **Cover Designer:** Karen Montgomery
Production Editor: Iris Febres   **Interior Designer:** David Futato
Proofreader: Iris Febres   **Illustrator:** Robert Romano

Revision History for the First Edition:
    2012-05-04   First release
See *http://oreilly.com/catalog/errata.csp?isbn=9781449320232* for release details.

ISBN: 978-1-449-32023-2

[LSI]

1336156818

Table of Contents

Preface

As you start to look at getting into mobile development, it can be overwhelming to try and choose between all the different options and platforms available to you. Each platform comes with its own set of tools, preferred languages, and overall way of doing things. In many cases, you won't want to restrict your application to a single platform, so naturally you'll start looking for ways to reuse your code across the different platforms. If you're a .NET developer, you are already in a great position, as you can actually leverage the .NET framework across iOS, Android, and Windows Phone, and hit the ground running on all of them.

This book will introduce you to all three platforms from the ground up, exploring how to write native applications for each of them. As part of this exploration, you will see how to perform some common tasks required by applications, such as accessing the network, finding the user's location, and persisting data on the device. In addition to learning about the platforms themselves, you will see how you can use .NET and C# to build these native applications, as well as various techniques for achieving a large amount of code reuse across all of them.

Who Is This Book For?

This book assumes that you are already familiar with the basics of the .NET Framework and the C# programming language. If you aren't already experienced in either of these, this book will still be useful, but I first suggest familiarizing yourself with the basics before diving in.

That said, this book does not assume any level of familiarity with mobile development prior to reading. If you're brand new to mobile development, or even if you're familiar with the platforms but are curious to see how to leverage C# across them, this book will walk you through everything you need in order to get started writing your applications.

Contents of This Book

Chapter 1
   Introduces the different platforms and options for developing applications for them

Chapter 2
   Walks you through setting up your environments and creating your first application on each platform

Chapter 3
   Presents several techniques to help maximize code reuse across each platform

Chapter 4
   Describes how to access network resources in your applications

Chapter 5
   Introduces several methods for saving data in an application, including the filesystem and local databases

Chapter 6
   Demonstrates how to access a user's location in an application, as well as how to use each platform's mapping APIs

Appendix A
   Explains how to customize Android virtual devices in order to emulate different device configurations

Appendix B
   Lists various resources for learning more about developing for each platform

Conventions Used in This Book

The following typographical conventions are used in this book:

Italic
   Indicates new terms, URLs, email addresses, filenames, and file extensions.

`Constant width`
   Used for program listings, as well as within paragraphs to refer to program elements such as variable or function names, databases, data types, environment variables, statements, and keywords.

`Constant width bold`
   Shows commands or other text that should be typed literally by the user.

`Constant width italic`
   Shows text that should be replaced with user-supplied values or by values determined by context.

This icon signifies a tip, suggestion, or general note.

This icon indicates a warning or caution.

This Book's Example Files

You can download all of the code examples from this book from the following locations:

http://github.com/gshackles/MobileDevelopmentInCSharpBook

http://examples.oreilly.com/0636920024002/

In the example files you will find the completed versions of the applications built in every chapter of the book, which will contain all the code required to run them.

Using Code Examples

This book is here to help you get your job done. In general, you may use the code in this book in your programs and documentation. You do not need to contact us for permission unless you're reproducing a significant portion of the code. For example, writing a program that uses several chunks of code from this book does not require permission. Selling or distributing a CD-ROM of examples from O'Reilly books does require permission. Answering a question by citing this book and quoting example code does not require permission. Incorporating a significant amount of example code from this book into your product's documentation does require permission.

We appreciate, but do not require, attribution. An attribution usually includes the title, author, publisher, and ISBN. For example: "*Mobile Development with C#* by Greg Shackles (O'Reilly). Copyright 2012 Greg Shackles, 978-1-449-32023-2."

If you feel your use of code examples falls outside fair use or the permission given above, feel free to contact us at *permissions@oreilly.com*.

Safari® Books Online

Safari Books Online (*www.safaribooksonline.com*) is an on-demand digital library that delivers expert content in both book and video form from the world's leading authors in technology and business.

Technology professionals, software developers, web designers, and business and creative professionals use Safari Books Online as their primary resource for research, problem solving, learning, and certification training.

Safari Books Online offers a range of product mixes and pricing programs for organizations, government agencies, and individuals. Subscribers have access to thousands of books, training videos, and prepublication manuscripts in one fully searchable database from publishers like O'Reilly Media, Prentice Hall Professional, Addison-Wesley Professional, Microsoft Press, Sams, Que, Peachpit Press, Focal Press, Cisco Press, John Wiley & Sons, Syngress, Morgan Kaufmann, IBM Redbooks, Packt, Adobe Press, FT Press, Apress, Manning, New Riders, McGraw-Hill, Jones & Bartlett, Course Technology, and dozens more. For more information about Safari Books Online, please visit us online.

How to Contact Us

Please address comments and questions concerning this book to the publisher:

O'Reilly Media, Inc.
1005 Gravenstein Highway North
Sebastopol, CA 95472
800-998-9938 (in the United States or Canada)
707-829-0515 (international or local)
707-829-0104 (fax)

We have a web page for this book, where we list errata, examples, and any additional information. You can access this page at:

http://www.oreilly.com/catalog/9781449320232

To comment or ask technical questions about this book, send email to:

bookquestions@oreilly.com

For more information about our books, courses, conferences, and news, see our website at *http://www.oreilly.com*.

Find us on Facebook: *http://facebook.com/oreilly*

Follow us on Twitter: *http://twitter.com/oreillymedia*

Watch us on YouTube: *http://www.youtube.com/oreillymedia*

Acknowledgments

There may be only one name listed on the cover, but this book is truly the product of the hard work of many people. First, I would like to thank O'Reilly for giving me the opportunity to write this book and for being great to work with. Specifically, I'd like to thank my editor, Rachel Roumeliotis, for making this book happen and providing plenty of help and feedback throughout the entire process.

I also had some top-notch technical reviewers to help me out: Miguel de Icaza and Jeff Blankenburg. Miguel de Icaza is a well-known figure in the software world, having started projects like GNOME and Mono, and is also the founder of Xamarin. I am extremely honored to have had him involved in writing this book. Without Miguel and his amazing team over at Xamarin, the Mono project, MonoTouch, and Mono for Android would never have happened. Jeff is a Developer Evangelist for Microsoft, and is an established authority and author in the realm of Windows Phone. Both Miguel and Jeff are experts in the field and provided invaluable feedback and suggestions that really helped shape the book you're reading right now.

Last but certainly not least, I want to thank my family and friends for their constant support. In particular, I'd like to thank Angie and Roger for putting up with me while I spent most of my time working, and for helping keep me sane along the way.

CHAPTER 1

Surveying the Landscape

The last decade has been nothing short of a whirlwind in the mobile space. Phones have been transformed from simple conveniences to indispensable extensions of everyday life. With high-resolution displays, GPS, cameras capable of both still photography and recording high-definition videos, full-featured web browsers, rich native applications, touchscreens, and a constant connection to the Internet, the phone has evolved into a powerful mobile computer. The evolution has gone so far that the actual telephone functionality has essentially become secondary to the rest of the features. Today's mobile phone is now more than the sum of its parts. It is your connection to the world.

The Players

As with any fast-moving market, there are many players with skin in the mobile game at any given time. This book, however, is going to be focused on three of the bigger names right now:

iOS

It can be argued that Apple is responsible for being the catalyst in bringing about the modern smartphone generation. Back in early 2007, Apple announced the iPhone, which marked the company's first foray into building their own mobile phone. The product included many features, such as a touchscreen and a focus on a polished user experience, that would quickly become standard in smartphones across the board. In many ways, the iPhone remains the gold standard for smartphones today, even as the market continues to evolve and innovate. Apple's mobile operating system, iOS, is also found on its tablet offering, the iPad, as well as the iPod, Apple's portable music player. Since the company produces both the devices and operating system, it maintains a high level of control over its ecosystem.

Android

Since Google purchased it in 2005 and began releasing versions in 2008, Android has taken the smartphone market by storm. Just a few years and numerous versions after its initial release, as of February 2012, Android accounts for just over 50% of the US smartphone market, a number that continues to climb every month (*http://www.com score.com/Press_Events/Press_Releases/2012/4/comScore_Reports_February_2012_U .S._Mobile_Subscriber_Market_Share*). Most of Android is open source and licensed in a way that gives hardware vendors a lot of flexibility, so the ecosystem of Android phones is very diverse. Because of that flexibility, many vendors make significant changes to the versions of Android that ship on their devices, so very few devices are actually running a stock version of the operating system. With the release of Honeycomb, Android has also started to stake its claim in the tablet market as well. Additionally, Android can be found in Google's television platform, Google TV, as well devices such as Barnes & Noble's Nook Color and Amazon's Kindle Fire, which bring the richness of tablets to the world of e-readers. Ice Cream Sandwich, the version of Android following Honeycomb, aims to help bridge the growing divide between Android smartphones and tablets.

Windows Phone

In 2010, Microsoft released Windows Phone 7, which marked a long-overdue shift away from its legacy Windows Mobile platform that had long since stagnated. The user interface in Windows Phone 7, dubbed Metro, is decidedly unlike the approach taken by both iOS and Android. A strong emphasis is placed on simplicity, typography, and expansive interfaces that aim to provide a sense of depth and a natural user experience. Device vendors are given a small amount of freedom in designing their devices, but Microsoft maintains a strict set of requirements they have to meet in order to ensure stability and quality, as well as avoid some of the fragmentation problems seen in the Android realm. While the platform is still in the very early stages of its life, Microsoft seems dedicated to pushing the platform forward to try and gain back some of the market share the company has lost over the years. In late 2011, Microsoft shipped the Windows Phone 7.5 update, codenamed Mango, which started to bring in many features missing from the first releases, such as local databases and camera access.

Write Once, Run Anywhere

iOS, Android, and Windows Phone, despite the fact that they are all mobile platforms, have very distinct ways of doing things and their own required languages in which to do them. iOS applications are written in Objective-C, while Android makes use of Java. Windows Phone leverages the .NET Framework, where the primary languages are C# and Visual Basic .NET. You can also use C and C++ on iOS and Android, but they are not currently supported on Windows Phone (see Table 1-1). As developers, we dread the idea of having to repeat all of our work three times in three different programming languages. Aside from the upfront overhead of doing the work three times, bug fixes found later on will also likely have to be fixed three times. For any non-trivial application, the technical debt can add up quickly, so the natural response is to seek out some sort of cross-platform solution to minimize the cost of building and maintaining applications for these devices.

Table 1-1. Native platform languages

	iOS	Android	Windows Phone
C / C++	X	X	
Objective-C	X		
Java		X	
C#			X
Visual Basic .NET			X

The promise of a "write once, run anywhere" solution is nothing new in the development world. It tends to come around whenever there's a need to publish applications on multiple platforms, whether on the desktop or on mobile devices. The mantra was originally coined by Sun when it was pushing for Java to be the unifying language for all platforms and devices. The concept is certainly not unique to Java, though, nor was that the first time such a solution was proposed.

It has a natural appeal to us as developers. Who wouldn't want a silver bullet like that at our disposal? We could write everything once, get it just the way we want it, and then instantly be able to target users on all platforms. Unfortunately, things that seem too good to be true often are; there's a reason why Java, over a decade and a half into its life, has yet to become the common language for developing cross-platform desktop applications. I think Nat Friedman, CEO of Xamarin, put it best in an interview he did on the .NET Rocks! podcast:

> "'Write once, run anywhere perfectly' is a unicorn."

Now, let me take a step back for just a moment to provide some clarification here. I don't intend for anything in this chapter, or this book for that matter, to be taken as a slight against frameworks that decided to take this approach to solving the problem. The silver bullet trap works in both directions. No matter the context, there is never a solution so perfect that it solves all problems. Instead, what I will outline in this book is meant to demonstrate only one approach to solving things. It's another set of tools for your developer tool belt.

Having said that, let's take a moment to think about who stands to benefit the most from the "write once, run anywhere" method. You could make the argument that the user benefits from you being quicker to market or supporting his platform, and though there is some legitimacy to that, I would tend to disagree. Instead, when all is said and done, it is we, the developers, who really benefit by cutting down the amount of time it takes to write and publish our applications. However, this reduced development time often involves making concessions that sacrifice user experience. Each platform has its own hardware configurations, with varying screen sizes, resolutions, and buttons. Each has its own set of user interaction metaphors and guidelines for how an application should look and behave. In order for your application to look and feel native, it should act like the other applications on that platform.

Writing to the lowest common denominator can end up making your application feel foreign to all of them. Applications on Windows Phone are designed to look and behave differently than those on iOS, and that is something that should be embraced rather than glossed over or abstracted away. The experience you present to your users should be the primary concern when designing your application's interface. Ultimately, that is what will set your application apart from others who take shortcuts along the way.

By now, you're probably thinking to yourself, "So if I'm not writing in the platform's native language, and I'm not leveraging one of these cross-platform frameworks, how do you expect me to write my applications?"

An Alternative Approach

What I am going to propose is an alternative approach where you can leverage the power of the .NET Framework, along with the powerful C# language, across all three platforms. While this may sound similar to "write once, run anywhere," the key difference is that C# and the Base Class Libraries are used as a universal language and library where the device-specific and user interface-specific elements are not abstracted, but are instead exposed to developers. This means that developers build native applications using three different user interface programming models, one for each platform, while using C# across the board.

As mentioned earlier, .NET is exposed natively on Windows Phone, so there's no friction there. However, we know that on both iOS and Android it is not, so how can we make this work? To help bridge this gap, a company named Xamarin has created two products, MonoTouch and Mono for Android. We will explore these products in more depth in later chapters, but the elevator pitch is that they allow for writing native applications in C# (see Table 1-2), providing bindings to the platform's native libraries and toolkits so that you're targeting the same classes you would in Objective-C for iOS or Java for Android. Because you're working against the platform's native user interface toolkits, you don't need to worry about how to make your application look and feel native to the platform, since it already is.

Table 1-2. Native platform languages with Mono tools

	iOS	Android	Windows Phone
C / C++	X	X	
Objective-C	X		

	iOS	Android	Windows Phone
Java		X	
C#	X	X	X
Visual Basic .NET			X

Apple is known for being strict about what gets into the App Store, so you might be wondering whether it will only accept applications written natively in Objective-C. There are actually thousands of MonoTouch applications in the store. In fact, iCircuit, a MonoTouch application, was shipped with their demo iPad 2 units that were sent out to stores.

As the names imply, MonoTouch and Mono for Android expose .NET on iOS and Android by leveraging Mono, an open-source, cross-platform implementation of the Common Language Infrastructure (CLI), an ISO standard that describes the virtual execution environment that is used by C#. Despite the fact that they are commercial products, both offer free evaluation versions that do not expire, and allow you to deploy to the iOS simulator or the Android emulator. There is no risk in taking them out for a spin. In the next chapter, we will explore how to get started with these tools, and build your first application along the way.

Apple and Google release new versions regularly, so you might be wondering what that means for you if you're using MonoTouch or Mono for Android. Generally, there is no waiting period here, as both products track the beta programs for iOS and Android. For example, MonoTouch typically releases the bindings for a new operating system within 24 hours of the official Apple release. In addition to the quick release cycle, Xamarin offers first-class support for its products, providing prompt responses through mailing lists and IRC, and maintaining thorough, user-friendly documentation. Even outside of Xamarin, the Mono community in general is very active and helpful as well. You can find information about the company and products at *http://www.xamarin.com/*.

If you're already a .NET developer, you can immediately hit the ground running, still having the familiar namespaces and classes in the Base Class Library at your disposal. Since the Mono Framework is being used to run your code, you don't need to worry about whether Objective-C or Java implements a particular C# feature you want to use. That means you get things like generics, LINQ to Objects, LINQ to XML, events, lambda expressions, reflection, garbage collection, thread pooling, and asynchronous programming features. Taking things even further, you can often leverage many existing third-party .NET libraries in your applications as well. You can turn your focus towards solving the business problem at hand instead of learning and fighting yet another set of new languages.

As great as this is, the bigger win with this approach is the ability to share a large percentage of your core application code across all platforms. The key to making the most out of this is to structure your applications in such a way that you extract your core business logic into a separate layer, independent of any particular user interface, and reference that across platforms. By doing so, each application essentially becomes a native user interface layer on top of that shared layer, so you get all the benefits of a native user experience without having to rewrite the application's main functionality every time (see Table 1-3). In Chapter 3, we will explore some techniques available to help keep as much code as possible in this shared layer and maximize code reuse across platforms.

Table 1-3. Application layers

	iOS	Android	Windows Phone
Runtime	Mono	Mono	.NET
Business logic	C#	C#	C#
User interface	MonoTouch	Mono for Android	Silverlight

The classes and methods exposed by a framework make up what is referred to as its *profile*. The .NET profile exposed by both MonoTouch and Mono for Android is based on the Mono Mobile profile. The mobile profile is a version of the .NET 4.0 API that has some of the desktop and server features removed for the sake of running on small embedded devices, such as the `System.Configuration` namespace. This profile is very similar to the core of Silverlight, which is also a subset of the full .NET profile for the same reasons. Since Windows Phone is also based on Silverlight, there is a large amount of overlap between all three of these profiles, meaning that non-user interface code you write for one platform is very likely to be compatible with the other two.

Technically, the Windows Phone platform supports developing applications using both the Silverlight and XNA frameworks. Since XNA is more suited for game development, this book will focus on building applications with Silverlight. By definition, games define their own user interfaces, so not all of the problems outlined earlier with regards to providing a quality cross-platform user experience will necessarily apply when developing games.

The MonoGame project provides an XNA 2D implementation that runs on both MonoTouch and Mono for Android. This is a third-party community project that is continuously evolving. More information about the MonoGame project can be found at *http://github.com/mono/MonoGame*.

In later chapters, we'll explore various patterns and techniques to help maximize the amount of functionality that can go into the shared layer. After walking through the process of creating a simple application for iOS, Android, and Windows Phone, we'll go through many of the common tasks you'll want to perform in your applications, such as consuming data from the Internet, persisting data to the filesystem or a database, and accessing the device's location information and mapping capabilities. As we go through these topics, we'll discuss how you can achieve some code reusability there as well.

It's also worth noting that since .NET is being used across the board, reusing code in this shared layer isn't just limited to mobile applications, or even just Silverlight-based applications. Since the Silverlight profile is essentially a subset of the full .NET Framework, in addition to Silverlight for the web or desktop, the same code can be applied to applications written in ASP.NET, WPF, Windows Forms, or even a Windows 8 Metro application. Using Mono, you can also take your code onto Linux or even the Mac using MonoMac, which takes a similar approach to MonoTouch and Mono for Android. In the end, your code can follow you anywhere the .NET Framework goes. That's pretty powerful.

Summary

In this chapter, we looked at some of the big names in the smartphone world and evaluated some of the options available to us as developers for building applications on these devices. We then explored how to target all three platforms using the .NET Framework, as well as the benefits this method brings with it. By using this approach, you can develop fully native applications across each platform without having to abstract away the user interface, while still being able to reuse the bulk of your code across them all. In the next chapter, we will walk through setting up your development environment and building your first application on all three platforms.

CHAPTER 2

Hello, Platforms!

Since you have to crawl before you can walk, this chapter will introduce each platform individually and create a simple application for each of them. Like all "Hello, World!" applications, the one you build in this chapter will be overly simplistic, consisting of just two screens. On the first screen will be a button labeled "Click Me!" When that is clicked, the application will navigate to a second screen, which will display text sent to it from the first screen. To keep things simple, it can just send and display the time at which the button was clicked. The goal of this chapter is to get your feet wet in each platform while taking a look at the pieces and environments involved in creating them.

iOS

Let's start with iOS, Apple's mobile operating system. The main prerequisite for doing iOS development, or any Apple-based development for that matter, is that you need to be running Mac OS X. This is a restriction set by Apple, so even though you will be using .NET to build the application, there is no getting around this limitation.

On top of the operating system, in order to get up and running with iOS development, you'll need to install these software packages:

- Xcode 4
- Mono Framework
- MonoDevelop
- MonoTouch

Xcode is Apple's Integrated Development Environment (IDE), and also includes other tools such as the iOS simulator, a user interface designer, and the SDKs for Mac OS X and iOS. It is available for download from either the OS X App Store or from Apple's iOS Dev Center if you've set up an account. Throughout this book, you won't be using Xcode itself all that much, but installing it is still a requirement. Instead, MonoDevelop will be the primary development environment for writing iOS applications.

MonoDevelop is a cross-platform, open source IDE, similar in style and capabilities to Microsoft's Visual Studio. To get started with iOS development with C#, you'll also need to install MonoTouch, which installs as a plug-in for MonoDevelop. Instructions and links for downloading all of these packages are available on Xamarin's website at *http://docs.xamarin.com/ios*.

What Is MonoTouch?

Before we go too far, let's step back and take a quick look at what MonoTouch is and how it works. MonoTouch is a development kit that allows developers to use C# to build iOS applications. MonoTouch provides a set of iOS-specific bindings to Apple's Cocoa Touch APIs that can be consumed from C#. In addition, MonoTouch also provides access to the .NET Base Class Library, including generics, garbage collection, LINQ, asynchronous programming patterns, delegates, and more.

The set of APIs exposed by the base class libraries have been fine-tuned for use in mobile scenarios. Components or features that were designed for powerful servers or desktop computing have been removed. iOS is an operating system designed for mobile devices having CPUs that have a fraction of the power of a desktop or server, and a fraction of the memory as well. This is why certain APIs, such as `System.Configuration` and all of its features, have been completely removed from MonoTouch.

This simplified profile is called the Mono Mobile profile. It was originally based on the Silverlight profile because Silverlight also had to remove many of the same server or desktop-specific components, as well as some components that were simply too big. The Mono Mobile profile grew out of this and added many of the new .NET 4.0 features along the way, such as the `System.Threading.Tasks` namespace. You can think of the Mono Mobile API as being somewhere between Silverlight and the full .NET 4.0 desktop APIs.

In most environments, code targeting the .NET framework is compiled into a *Common Intermediate Language (CIL)*, which is then compiled into native code at runtime using a *Just in Time (JIT)* compiler. However, Apple made the decision to prohibit Just in Time compilation in iOS, meaning that this approach is not possible. To work around this limitation, MonoTouch includes an *Ahead of Time (AOT)* compiler that compiles your application down to native code at build time, generating the same ARM machine code that a JIT compiler would have generated at runtime.

While a vast majority of the .NET runtime is supported, there are some limitations that come as a side effect of using an Ahead of Time compiler. Any code that depends upon runtime code generation cannot be supported. For example, although reflection is supported, `Reflection.Emit` is not, since its output could not be determined at compile time. Other limitations include uses of Generics that cannot be fully resolved at compile time. A complete list of the limitations of MonoTouch is available at *http://docs.xamarin.com/ios/about/limitations*.

Since iOS does not support system-wide runtime or libraries, your application needs to bundle every library that it consumes, including any components from MonoTouch that you use. Naturally, you don't want to have to ship the entire .NET framework— with every application—to these devices, where resources are very limited, especially when the application likely only uses a small subset of that framework. To solve this problem, MonoTouch ships with a *linker*. The linker is a static analysis tool that goes through each assembly and strips out any code that isn't actually used in the application.

As you can imagine, this helps to cut down application size significantly. For example, if your application only used the `Console.WriteLine` method, this method and any other dependencies are the only ones that will be included in the final executable. The linker basically traces all of the referenced types and members and ensures that everything that your code uses is included.

Sometimes you might want to force the linker to include some code in cases where it might have otherwise excluded it. This can happen if you have parts of your code that are not explicitly referenced, but are still required for the application to function properly. In these cases, you can also use the `[MonoTouch.Foundation.Preserve]` attribute to tell the linker not to remove a class or its members in situations where you might not be referencing them explicitly in your code, such as during serialization.

Memory management is an area where .NET and Objective-C differ quite a bit. Objects in .NET are managed by the garbage collector, which automatically determines when it is safe to release the memory used by an object. In Objective-C, objects are retain counted, which requires more work during development to allocate and release references to objects manually. The retain count of an object represents the number of other objects that have registered interest in it, meaning that it should be kept in memory. Once an object's retain count reaches zero, iOS will free up that memory so it can be reused. MonoTouch abstracts this system away for you, bringing along garbage collection to iOS development and making memory management much simpler.

Although the garbage collector will do its work, it might not perform a garbage collection or release memory immediately. This is why many classes in MonoTouch implement the `IDisposable` interface. This interface is implemented to allow developers to call its `Dispose` method, explicitly releasing resources before the garbage collector gets a chance to run. Since iOS runs on devices with very limited resources, some re-

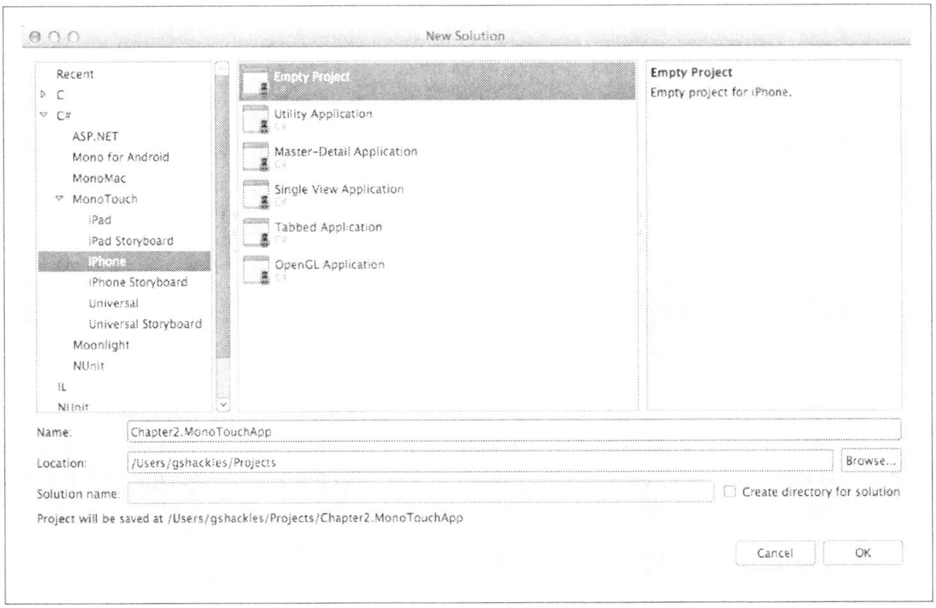

Figure 2-1. Create a new application

sources need to be treated as being very precious and should be disposed of as soon as possible. For example, a full-screen image on an iPhone 3GS can use about 600 KB of memory, due to a screen resolution of 320x480 and a memory usage of 4 bytes per pixel. Starting with the iPhone 4, Apple doubled the screen resolution, meaning that full-screen images will require twice that amount of memory.

Objective-C also has a feature called *protocols* that is similar to interfaces in .NET. Like interfaces, protocols define a list of methods that a class can implement, and a class can implement any number of protocols. The main difference is that methods in a protocol are optional, so MonoTouch binds them to abstract classes with virtual methods. Unfortunately, it's not a perfect translation, as C# does not support multiple inheritance. One common application of protocols is found in Objective-C's use of the delegation pattern, in which a class can ask another class, the *delegate*, to do some work for it. The delegate class implements the protocol that the calling class wants done. This scenario is typically handled by events in .NET, so in many cases MonoTouch will actually expose events that abstract away the delegate classes to make it easier to consume with C# code and also help get around the lack of multiple inheritance.

Create the Application

You are now ready to create your first iOS application. Fire up MonoDevelop and create a new solution by clicking File→New→Solution from the application menus. Select iPhone→Empty Project and name it Chapter2.MonoTouchApp, as shown in Figure 2-1.

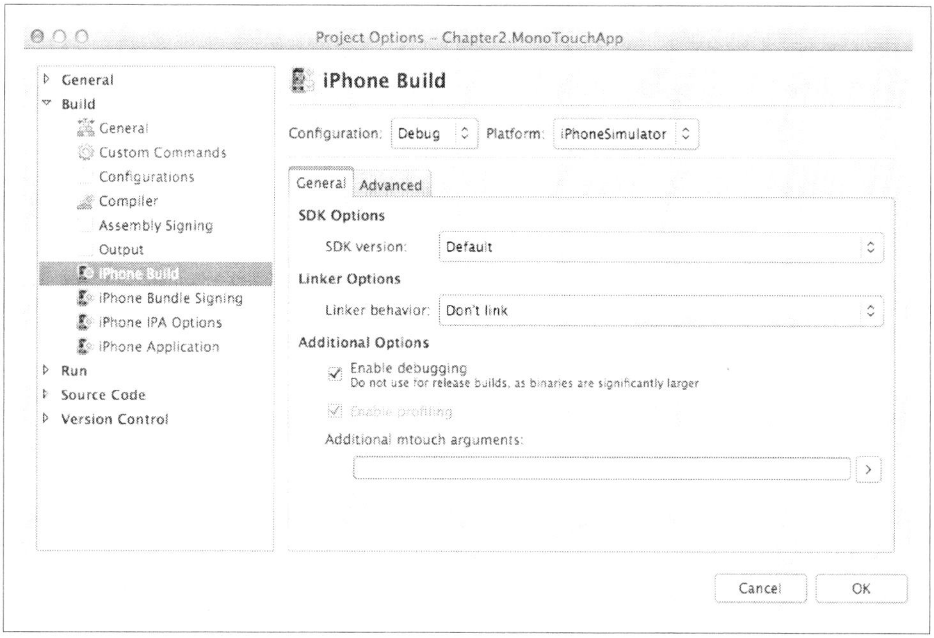

Figure 2-2. Build options for the application

Now you should be looking at a new solution, containing three files:

AppDelegate.cs
    A delegate class used to manage the lifecycle of the application

Main.cs
    Entry point of the application that starts the application delegate

Info.plist
    Contains configuration items for the application

If you double-click on the project in the solution explorer, or select the Project→Chapter2.MonoTouchApp Options menu item, you'll see the properties dialog for the application. On the left side of this dialog, you'll find sections with labels prefixed with "iPhone" that allow you to configure various aspects of the application. For example, Figure 2-2 shows the "iPhone Build" options, which allow you to configure the SDK version you want to use, as well as which assemblies you want the linker to operate on.

Defining the Interface

The first thing that we need to do is create the screens of our application. iOS applications follow the *Model View Controller (MVC)* pattern, where each screen has a corresponding *view* that represents the piece visible to the user, as well as a *view controller* that manages its lifecycle and events. Right click on the project, choose

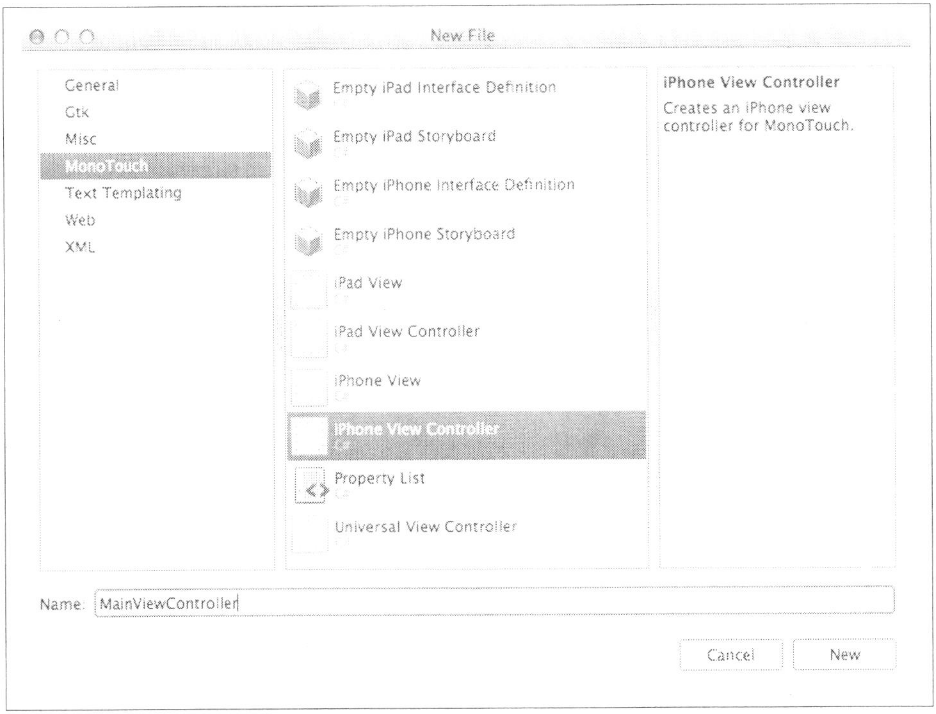

| General | Empty iPad Interface Definition | iPhone View Controller |
| Gtk | Empty iPad Storyboard | Creates an iPhone view controller for MonoTouch. |

Figure 2-3. *Add a new view controller to the project*

Add→New File, and add a new iPhone View Controller named `MainViewController`, as shown in Figure 2-3. Repeat this process once more to create another view controller named `SecondViewController`.

Model View Controller is an architectural pattern designed to decouple the user interface of an application from the underlying logic to allow for more flexibility and make it easier to maintain the application in the future. The "view" refers to the part of the application that the user sees and interacts with. The "model" here is the underlying data of the application. It is independent of the interface and is responsible for maintaining state and the behavior of the system. A "controller" handles all communication between the model and the view so that they don't interact directly. The MVC pattern is found in many areas, and has especially taken hold in web frameworks such as ASP.NET MVC and Ruby on Rails.

For each of these view controllers, you'll find three files added to the project. In addition to the main C# class file, there is an XIB file, containing the view definition, and a designer file that contains any hooks we define to allow the controller to access elements in the view. XIB files are editable through Xcode's Interface Builder, a graphical tool provided by Apple for creating user interfaces for your applications. Double-click on *MainViewController.xib*, which should launch Xcode and load the view into Interface Builder (see Figure 2-4).

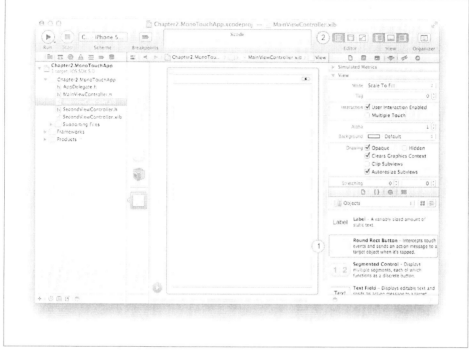

Figure 2-4. Xcode's Interface Builder

This screen just needs a single button labeled "Click Me!" From the library pane in the lower right portion of Interface Builder, labeled as #1 in Figure 2-4, click and drag a button onto the view surface, placing it wherever you like. You can resize the button by selecting it and then dragging the handles to get the size you want. To change the button's text, double-click on it and then enter the text "Click Me!" You can find many other options to customize the view, such as changing the font and text color, on the right when you have the button selected.

Now that the button is defined, we need to create a way for the view controller to get access to it in code. There are two ways to expose elements from the view: *outlets* and *actions*. Outlets allow you to expose the UI element itself as a property that can be accessed from your C# code. In order to make this connection, MonoTouch will add outlets to the class designer file mentioned earlier. Actions connect specific events of an element to a method that is invoked in response to it. For example, you can create an action for the event fired when a button is tapped, rather than expose the entire button from the view. Since Interface Builder is hardwired to edit Objective-C code,

MonoTouch will generate a mirror of all of your C# code and your UI into an Xcode project to allow you to use the tool.

In order to define this view's connections, start by showing the Assistant Editor in Interface Builder: select the middle option in the toolbar above Editor, labeled as #2 in Figure 2-4. This will tell Interface Builder to show both the view and the generated Objective-C header file for the view controller. This header file, *MainViewController.h*, is what MonoTouch watches in order to generate the designer file for the classes: *MainViewController.designer.cs*. For the sake of demonstration, we will define both an outlet and an action for the button.

To create the outlet, hold down the Control key, click on the button and then drag it inside of the interface definition within the header file. When Interface Builder prompts you to define the connection, choose Outlet, name it `Button`, and leave the Type as `UIButton`. If this worked correctly, the code in the header file should now look like Example 2-1:

Example 2-1. MainViewController.h

```
#import <UIKit/UIKit.h>
#import <Foundation/Foundation.h>
#import <CoreGraphics/CoreGraphics.h>

@interface MainViewController : UIViewController {
}
@property (retain, nonatomic) IBOutlet UIButton *Button;

@end
```

We'll also create an action for when the button is tapped, which is very similar to defining an outlet. Just as with the outlet, click on the button while holding down the Control key and drag the button inside of the interface definition, which is contained in the header file. This time, select Action as the connection type, naming it `ButtonTapped`. There are many events to which you can choose to bind this action. The most common one you will use for a button is the "Touch Up Inside" event. This event doesn't get fired until the user picks takes her finger off the button, giving her a chance to cancel the action first. This will help keep your button's behavior consistent with how buttons behave in other iOS applications. That's the behavior we want for this application as well, so select that from the list of available events and click the "Connect" button.

Example 2-2. MainViewController.h (updated)

```
#import <UIKit/UIKit.h>
#import <Foundation/Foundation.h>
#import <CoreGraphics/CoreGraphics.h>

@interface MainViewController : UIViewController {
}
```

```
@property (retain, nonatomic) IBOutlet UIButton *Button;
- (IBAction)ButtonTapped:(id)sender;

@end
```

That's it for the first screen. Double-click on *SecondViewController.xib* to load that
view into Interface Builder. This time, instead of a button, we are going to create two
labels in the view. Choose "label" from the library pane on the right, and double-click
it to change the text to "Received Text:". Now take another label and place it directly
below the first one, setting the text to "(text)" as a placeholder so we can see it in the
designer, since the actual text will be assigned in code later on. Create an outlet for this
second label the same way you did for the first view, naming it ReceivedText and leaving
the Type set to UILabel. The code in the header file should look like Example 2-3:

Example 2-3. SecondViewController.h

```
#import <UIKit/UIKit.h>
#import <Foundation/Foundation.h>
#import <CoreGraphics/CoreGraphics.h>

@interface SecondViewController : UIViewController {
}
@property (retain, nonatomic) IBOutlet UILabel *ReceivedText;

@end
```

Writing the Application Code

That's everything you need to do in Interface Builder, so now switch back to
MonoDevelop. If you open up *MainViewController.designer.cs* (see Example 2-4) you'll
notice that items were added for the button's outlet and action that you created. The
outlet is added as a UIButton property, and the action is declared as a partial method.
In C#, partial methods allow you to define a method's signature in one part of a partial
class, and define the implementation in another. If you do not supply the implementation, the method and calls to it are removed during compilation. This lets Mono-
Touch to declare the signature for the ButtonTapped action in the generated designer
file, while allowing you to provide the implementation separately in your view controller code, as you will see later.

Example 2-4. MainViewController.designer.cs

```
using MonoTouch.Foundation;

namespace Chapter2.MonoTouchApp
{
    [Register ("MainViewController")]
    partial class MainViewController
    {
        [Outlet]
        MonoTouch.UIKit.UIButton Button { get; set; }
```

```
        [Action ("ButtonTapped:")]
        partial void ButtonTapped (MonoTouch.Foundation.NSObject sender);
    }
}
```

The first thing to do is tell the application to load the first screen when it starts up. To
do that, open up *AppDelegate.cs*, and modify it to look like Example 2-5:

Example 2-5. AppDelegate.cs

```
using MonoTouch.Foundation;
using MonoTouch.UIKit;

namespace Chapter2.MonoTouchApp
{
    [Register ("AppDelegate")]
    public partial class AppDelegate : UIApplicationDelegate
    {
        private UIWindow _window;
        private UINavigationController _navigationController;

        public override bool FinishedLaunching(UIApplication app, NSDictionary options) ❶
        {
            _window = new UIWindow (UIScreen.MainScreen.Bounds);

            _navigationController = new UINavigationController(); ❷
            _navigationController.PushViewController(new MainViewController(), false); ❸

            _window.RootViewController = _navigationController; ❹

            _window.MakeKeyAndVisible ();

            return true;
        }
    }
}
```

❶ Hook into the callback fired when the application finishes launching.

❷ Create a new instance of a UINavigationController. This is a type of view controller
that is part of Cocoa Touch that handles navigation between screens when you want
to allow the user to drill into hierarchical content. Alternatively, we could have added
a UINavigationController directly to the view in Interface Builder, but instead we
are instantiating it in code.

❸ Push the first screen into the controller. The second parameter to
PushViewController specifies whether the transition should be animated or not, and
no animation is needed for the initial view. This method is used whenever you want
to navigate to a new screen from within the UINavigationController.

❹ Finally, set the controller as the window's view, and then make it visible.

You may have noticed that many of the Cocoa Touch classes used so far are prefixed with "UI," such as UIApplicationDelegate, UIView Controller, and UIButton. The reason for this is that Objective-C doesn't support namespaces, so instead it makes use of prefixing in order to organize classes. MonoTouch keeps these class names the same to make it easier to translate between C# and Objective-C. When you're working with it, you can essentially think of UIViewController as being a class named ViewController that lives inside a namespace named UI.

Open up *MainViewController.cs* and replace the code that was generated by the MonoTouch template with the code in Example 2-6. There are many different lifecycle methods that you can override, depending on what you want to do, such as when the screen orientation is changing or when the view is shown to the user. The most common starting point for your view controller is ViewDidLoad(), which is called once the corresponding view has finished loading and all of its outlets and views have been instantiated—i.e., it's safe to start modifying it.

Example 2-6. MainViewController.cs

```
using System;
using MonoTouch.Foundation;
using MonoTouch.UIKit;

namespace Chapter2.MonoTouchApp
{
    public partial class MainViewController : UIViewController
    {
        public MainViewController() : base ("MainViewController", null)
        {
        }

        public override void ViewDidLoad() ❶
        {
            base.ViewDidLoad ();

            Title = "Hello, iOS!"; ❷

            Button.SetTitleColor(UIColor.Red, UIControlState.Normal); ❸
        }

        partial void ButtonTapped(NSObject sender) ❹
        {
            NavigationController.PushViewController( ❺
                new SecondViewController(DateTime.Now.ToLongTimeString()), true);
        }
    }
}
```

❶ Once the view has been loaded it is safe to start making changes.

❷ Set the title to be "Hello, iOS!" This text will show up in the title bar of the navigation controller when the application is run.

❸ Set the title color of the button to red for its normal state using the outlet defined in Interface Builder. This will make the button's text show up as red when it is loaded.

❹ In order to handle the ButtonTapped action defined in Interface Builder, provide an implementation for the partial method.

❺ When the button is tapped, navigate to a new instance of SecondViewController, passing in a string representing the current time and animating the transition.

Finally, open up *SecondViewController.cs* and remove any template code as you did with the first view controller. In MainViewController we passed in a string to Second ViewController through the constructor, so you'll need to create that constructor now. Once the view is ready, set the label's text to the text received in the constructor (see Example 2-7). The view is not ready for modification at the time the constructor is called, which is why it is saved in the class until the view is loaded.

Example 2-7. SecondViewController.cs

```
using MonoTouch.UIKit;

namespace Chapter2.MonoTouchApp
{
    public partial class SecondViewController : UIViewController
    {
        private readonly string _text;

        public SecondViewController(string text)
            : base ("SecondViewController", null)
        {
            _text = text; ❶
        }

        public override void ViewDidLoad()
        {
            base.ViewDidLoad ();

            Title = "Second View";

            ReceivedText.Text = _text; ❷
        }
    }
}
```

❶ Store the text sent in to the constructor so it can be used in the view.

❷ Update the label's text to the value passed into the constructor.

Now the application is ready to go! Select Run→Run from the application's menu, which should launch the application in the iOS simulator and look like Figure 2-5. You've now built your first iOS application!

The iOS simulator can be very nice to work with, but there are some things to be aware of as you're using it. Since it is a simulator, it has the same memory and computational capabilities as your local computer, both of which will certainly exceed that of a real device. This also means that JIT compilation will be possible within the simulator, but will fail on an actual device. One other difference is that filenames are case sensitive on a device, but not in the simulator, because Mac OS X is case insensitive. The simulator provides a good starting point, but there is no guarantee that an app that performs well in the simulator will run well on a device.

Figure 2-5. The application running in the simulator

Android

Now we can move on to building the Android version of the application. Unlike iOS, Android development can be done on either Windows or Mac OS X. In order to get started, you need to have the following software installed on your computer:

- Java JDK
- Android SDK
- MonoDevelop or Visual Studio 2010
- Mono for Android

If you're developing on Mac OS X you can use the MonoDevelop IDE, which you saw previously in the iOS example. If you're on Windows, you have the option of using either MonoDevelop or Microsoft's Visual Studio 2010. Xamarin provides a very useful all-in-one installer package that will download and install many of these prerequisites for you, which can make it much easier to get started. The most up-to-date instructions on how to install and configure all of these prerequisites are available on Xamarin's website at *http://docs.xamarin.com/android*. The installer will create several emulator images with which you may test out your applications, but you are free to modify them or create new ones according to what you need. Refer to Appendix A for how to manage Android's virtual devices.

 In order to use Mono for Android with Visual Studio, you must have one of the full versions of Visual Studio 2010 installed. Visual Studio 2010 Express doesn't expose the plug-in architecture required to make Mono for Android work. If you're on Windows and don't have a full Visual Studio license, MonoDevelop is available for free.

Mono for Android

Now that the Android tools are all set up, let's take a moment to talk about what Mono for Android is and what it brings to the table. Like MonoTouch did for iOS, Mono for Android provides .NET bindings to the Android APIs, which are mostly written in Java. Mono for Android also brings with it the .NET Base Class Library, based on the Mono Mobile profile, bringing in support for generics, LINQ, etc. The .NET profile exposed by Mono for Android is based on the same profile exposed by MonoTouch, so the main differences between them are just in the bindings to the native platforms. In addition, Mono for Android includes the same linker functionality described in the MonoTouch section, allowing you to ship only the bits of the .NET framework that you actually use. This will keep your application size down.

One main difference between MonoTouch and Mono for Android is that, unlike iOS, Android allows for Just in Time (JIT) compilation. Mono for Android will actually spin up an instance of the Mono runtime inside of your application's process when it starts

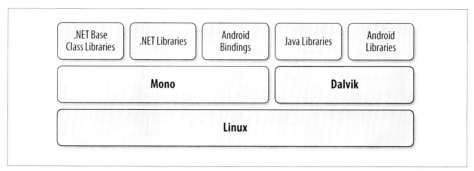

Figure 2-6. Mono for Android Architecture

up, and all .NET code will run directly against that. This allows you to access features that require runtime code generation, such as `Reflection.Emit`, which were not available in MonoTouch.

Standard Android applications are typically written in Java and run on Dalvik, Android's *JVM (Java Virtual Machine)*. This is a different virtual machine than what you may be familiar with from running Java on the desktop, and is more optimized for small devices where power consumption and memory constraints are important. In a Mono for Android application, the Mono runtime sits at the same architectural level as the Dalvik virtual machine (see Figure 2-6), where each is running directly on top of the underlying Linux kernel. In order to handle communication between the different runtimes, Mono for Android generates *callable wrappers*, which act as proxies for any class that inherits from `Java.Lang.Object`.

Mono for Android's garbage collector is also optimized for keeping track of objects that are referenced in both runtimes. This ensures that objects aren't collected prematurely. All objects that are derived from the `Java.Lang.Object` class, which includes all classes that are part of the Java and Android bindings, also implement the `IDisposable` interface. This allows you to invoke the object's `Dispose` method, which removes the tie to the reference in the Java runtime, allowing it to be garbage collected and free up resources.

Since the Android API is designed for Java, many aspects of it are built around that language. As such, some things simply don't transfer well over to C#, both in implementation style and in actual language support. For example, public variables of a class in Java are generally accessed and updated via getter and setter methods, such as `getName()` and `setName()`. In .NET, the convention is to make use of properties to provide that functionality. Mono for Android actually translates these cases so that if a Java class exposes `getName()` and `setName()` methods, Mono for Android will expose them through a `Name` property on the class instead.

Another example is Android's use of listener interfaces in order to handle events. In Java, to handle a button's click event, you would create an implementation of the listener interface for that event (see Example 2-8). However, this style does not translate well to C#, which does not support anonymous class implementations. Instead, in .NET, the convention is to use events to add and manage listeners, so Mono for Android exposes these scenarios as events.

Example 2-8. Handling a button click in Java

```
button.setOnClickListener(
    new View.OnClickListener()
    {
        @Override
        public void onClick(View v)
        {
            // handle click event
        }
    });
```

Example 2-9 shows two methods for handling the same button click event in C# and Mono for Android. In the first method, a *lambda expression* is used to handle the event. A lambda expression allows you to create an anonymous delegate to use for the event callback. It is useful for cases where the code needed in the callback is short, or for when it needs access to variables in the surrounding scope. For example, the code inside the lambda expression here will have access to the `message` variable passed into the `setupHandlers` method. In the second method, a separate method is assigned for handling the event. This style is useful when you want to share this method with other events, or for large methods that do not need any variables from the current scope.

Example 2-9. Two methods of handling a button click event in C#

```
void setupHandlers(string message)
{
    // Method 1: use a lambda expression
    button.Click += (sender, args) =>
    {
        // handle click event
    };

    // Method 2: assign a method to handle the event
    button.Click += handleClickEvent;
}

void handleClickEvent(object sender, EventArgs args)
{
    // handle click event
}
```

In Android applications, there is a lot of XML configuration required, such as declaring each component of your application, setting the target platform version, and requesting permissions. As you'll see once you start building applications, Mono for Android exposes most of this configuration through the project's property dialogs, as well as providing attributes to decorate your classes which generate the configuration during compilation. Most of the time, Mono for Android will be able to generate all of the

XML configuration you will need for your application, saving you from having to manage that yourself.

Create the Application

Although the examples in this section will primarily use Visual Studio 2010 on Windows, the process is almost identical when using MonoDevelop on either Windows or Mac. Create a new solution by clicking File→New Project in Visual Studio, or File→New→Solution in MonoDevelop. Select Mono for Android→Mono for Android Application and name it Chapter2.MonoAndroidApp, as shown in Figure 2-7.

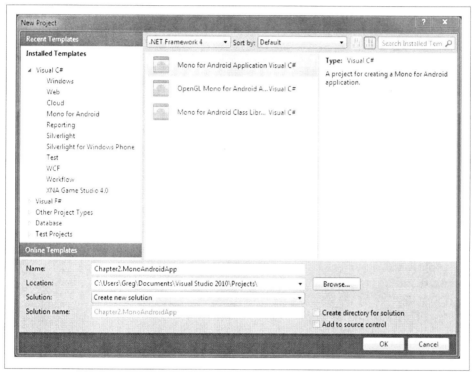

Figure 2-7. Create a new application

If you look in the project's properties, you'll find two configuration tabs named Android Manifest and Mono Android Options. In Android applications there is a file named *AndroidManifest.xml* that contains all configuration for the application, including component registration, permissions, and target versions. Much of what you would want to put in that file can be generated for you by using the Android Manifest options here (see Figure 2-8). In fact, more often than not, you'll never need to edit that file manually.

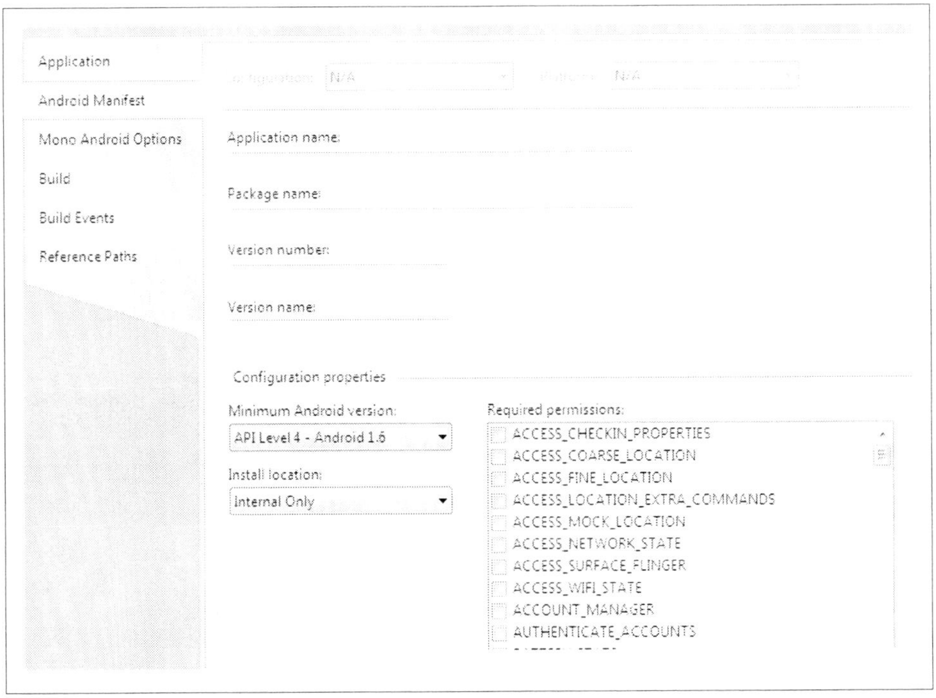

Figure 2-8. Android Manifest options

In your fresh Mono for Android solution, you should see these files and folders:

Assets
> This folder can be used to include raw assets in your application such as fonts. In order to tell Mono for Android that a file in this folder should be treated as an asset, make sure to set its Build Action property to *AndroidAsset*.

Resources
> This folder will contain different kinds of resources used by your application, such as layouts and images. Resources will be described in more depth in the next section.

Activity1.cs
> This is an activity provided with new Mono for Android applications that demonstrates some basic demo behavior. Activities will be explored more in the section "Writing the Application Code" on page 17.

Resources

The *Resources* folder is where you will put any resources that your application requires, organized into the appropriate folders. Pretty much anything that isn't actual application code will be filed under this folder, including view layout definitions, images, audio and video files, style definitions, and even localization strings. Mono for

Android uses the exact same resources as a Java Android application would, so any resources taken from an Android application written in Java can be used without modification.

During compilation, all of your resources will be run through Android's resource tools and the *Resource.Designer.cs* file will be generated which can also be found in the *Resources* folder. This file contains integer constants for all of your resources, which you will use in your application to access them. For example, if there is a resource file named *Main.xml* under the *Layout* folder, the designer file would contain code similar to Example 2-10. The actual value of the integer is subject to change, but that is not something you need to worry about as an application developer.

Example 2-10. Resource.Designer.cs

```
public partial class Resource
{
    public partial class Layout
    {
        // aapt resource value: 0x7f030000
        public const int Main = 2130903040;

        private Layout()
        {
        }
    }
}
```

At first it may seem odd to have to reference your resources using an integer identifier rather than simply providing a file path and name. The reason for this is that Android defines naming conventions on its resource folders that allow you to specify different versions of a resource. Android will decide at runtime which version of a resource to use based on the device and the criteria you specify. Even if you provide multiple versions of a resource, there will still be just one integer constant defined for it in Resource class. You can customize resources based on language, whether the device is in portrait or landscape mode, screen size, screen density, the version of Android, and much more.

In the default project template, you will see three resource folders defined for you:

Drawable
> This folder contains resources which can be drawn on the screen, including icons, images and shapes. Initially this folder contains an image resource, *Icon.png*, which is used as the application's icon.

Layout
> The user interface for a view in Android is typically defined in XML and located in this folder. By default there is a sample layout named *Main.axml*.

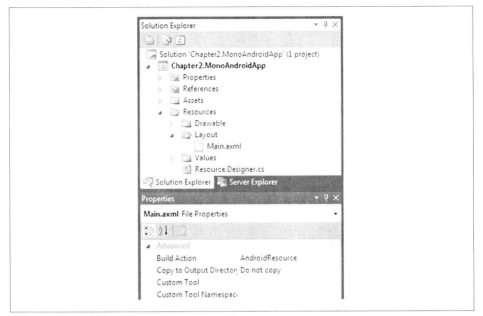

Figure 2-9. Setting a resource's Build Action

Values

> This folder is used for resources that contain values for an application, such as strings, arrays, and styles. This folder will initially contain a *Strings.xml* file that can be used for storing string constants used by your application.

The *Resource.Designer.cs* file only gets generated at compile time, so you will have to recompile your project to get it to reflect any resource changes you make. As part of the build process your resource files will be parsed by Android's resource tools, which can sometimes produce errors if there is a problem, such as invalid layout XML. If any errors are encountered during this step Mono for Android will bubble them up to you as build errors.

 In order to tell Mono for Android to treat a file as a resource, make sure to set its Build Action to *AndroidResource* in the file's properties (see Figure 2-9). If you find that your resource file isn't being processed or made accessible from the Resource class after a build where there were no build errors, odds are that you need to update the build action and recompile.

Defining the Interface

Now that the basics of Android are out of the way, let's get started building our application! To start from a clean slate, delete any files the default project template

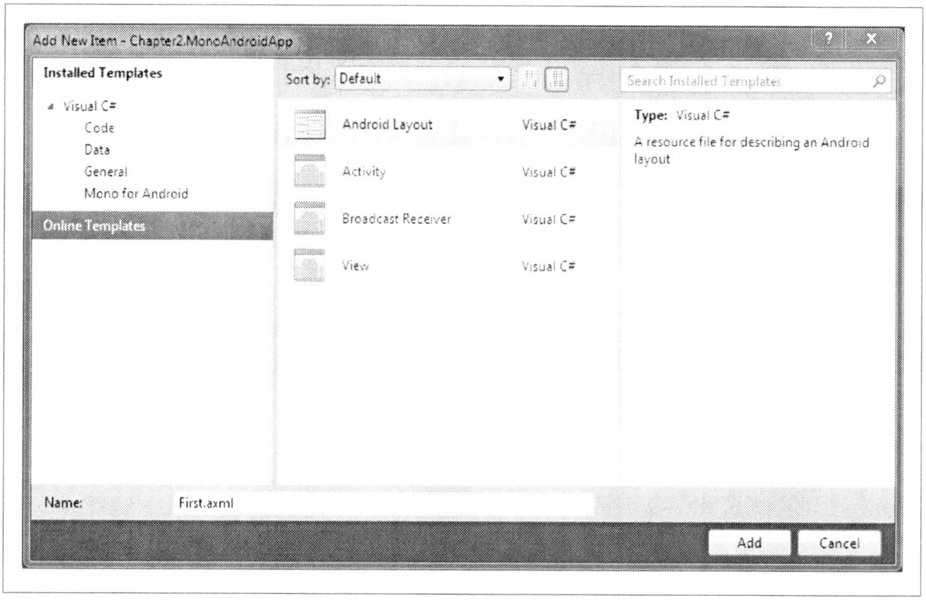

Figure 2-10. Creating a new layout

added in the *Layout* and *Values* folders, and also delete *Activity1.cs*. Next, right-click on the Layout folder, click Add→New Item, select Mono for Android→Android Layout and name it *First.axml* (see Figure 2-10).

> If you're using MonoDevelop the file will be named *First.xml*. The *AXML* extension is used to allow Visual Studio to provide some basic code completion when editing the file by associating it with a custom XML schema provided by Mono for Android. This is the only difference between the *AXML* and *XML* extensions, so everything else will behave the same regardless of which you use.

If you recall from the iOS application, the first screen in the application will contain just a single button labeled "Click Me!" Every element in a layout must specify the `layout_width` and `layout_height` attributes, which can be set to either `fill_parent` (renamed to `match_parent` in API level 8 and higher) or `wrap_content`. These attributes declare how to size the element inside its container. Specifying `fill_parent` or `match_parent` will cause the element to expand in that direction to take up as much space as its parent allows, while `wrap_content` will expand it only as far as its content requires. Update the layout XML to look like Example 2-11:

Example 2-11. First.axml

```
<?xml version="1.0" encoding="utf-8"?>
<LinearLayout xmlns:android="http://schemas.android.com/apk/res/android" ❶
    android:orientation="vertical"
```

```
    android:layout_width="fill_parent"
    android:layout_height="fill_parent">
  <Button  ❷
      android:id="@+id/Button"
      android:layout_width="fill_parent"
      android:layout_height="wrap_content"
      android:text="Click Me!" />
</LinearLayout>
```

❶ LinearLayout is used here as a container, which is a simple layout in which elements are stacked, either vertically or horizontally, one after the other.

❷ Create the button, setting its text to "Click Me!" and assigning it an ID so it can be referenced from code later on.

That's all you need for the first view, so go ahead and add a new layout named *Second.axml*. Inside the layout will be two TextView elements, one used as a label and another that will be updated from code (see Example 2-12). Note that you only need to define IDs on elements that you need programmatic access to.

Example 2-12. Second.axml

```
<?xml version="1.0" encoding="utf-8"?>
<LinearLayout xmlns:android="http://schemas.android.com/apk/res/android"  ❶
    android:orientation="vertical"
    android:layout_width="fill_parent"
    android:layout_height="fill_parent">

  <TextView  ❷
      android:layout_width="fill_parent"
      android:layout_height="wrap_content"
      android:paddingBottom="5dip"
      android:text="Received text: "/>

  <TextView  ❸
      android:id="@+id/Text"
      android:layout_width="fill_parent"
      android:layout_height="wrap_content" />

</LinearLayout>
```

❶ Use another LinearLayout so that the items will be stacked vertically.

❷ Create the label, setting its text and providing a small amount of padding on the bottom to space things out.

❸ Define the second TextView, assigning it an ID so we can set the value in code.

As you're writing these layouts manually, you might find yourself wondering about graphical designers for creating user interfaces. Sadly, the story there is currently lacking. Over on the Java side, if you're using the Eclipse IDE, you have access to a basic designer, which is certainly better than nothing. Unfortunately, there is currently no equivalent on the Mono for Android side. Since resource files are the same between Java and Mono for Android applications, you can still use the Eclipse designer, or any other Android layout designer, to experiment by copying the layout between IDEs. At least for the time being, you're likely to end up writing your layouts by hand.

When specifying the bottom padding on the label `TextView`, you may have noticed that it was done using a unit of measurement called `dip`, which stands for *density-independent pixels*. Android devices come in many different screen sizes and resolutions, which makes specifying layouts using physical pixels very difficult. Instead of having to do that, Android provides this unit of measurement you can use to help make it easier to scale across many screen sizes. You should always be sure to use density-independent pixels when declaring your user interfaces to avoid running into issues when running on different devices.

Writing the Application Code

That's all you need for the layouts, so let's move on to writing some code to wire them up. Android applications are made up of a handful of main building blocks, the most common of which is an *activity*. An activity is a single screen within an application, but its design is somewhat different than you may be used to on other platforms. In Android, an activity is meant to behave as a single standalone task that can conceivably be even be used by an entirely different application wanting to perform the same task.

The flow of an application is defined by starting activities based on what the user wants to do, independent of which application actually provides that activity. For example, if the user clicks on a URL in your application and wants to open it up in a web browser, you can simply tell Android to use the system's default web browser activity to handle this, instead of having to reinvent the wheel and do this yourself. In general, there is only one activity running on a device at any given time.

So if activities are largely independent pieces of an application, how do they tie together to form a cohesive application? That's where *intents* come into play. Intents are messages you create that tell Android what you'd like to do next, such as starting a new activity. Intents fall into two main categories: explicit and implicit. With explicit intents, you know exactly which component you'd like to activate, such as when you launch another activity within your own application.

Implicit intents are where the decoupled nature of activities gets its power. You can specify in your intent the type of task you'd like to perform, and Android will route that message to an application that registered that it can handle the request. If there are multiple applications eligible to handle the request, the user is able to decide which he would like to use.

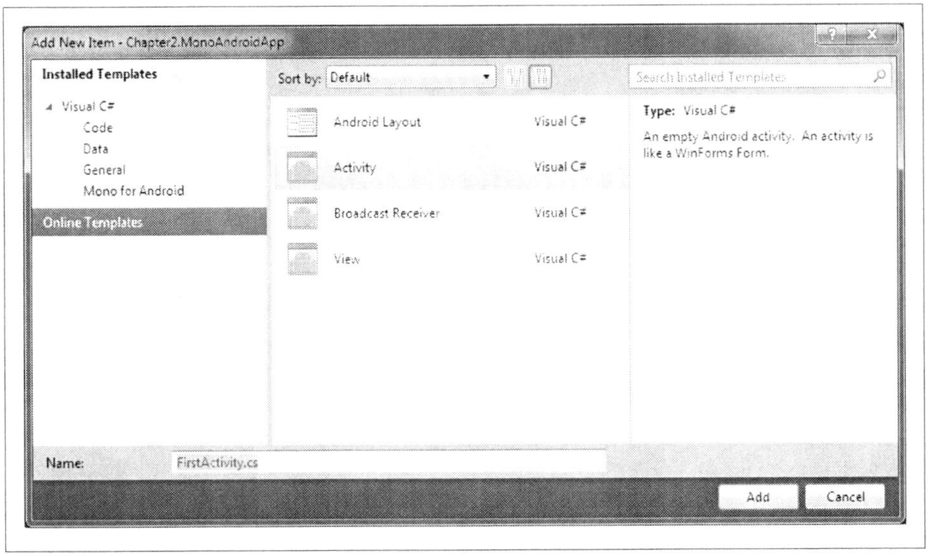

Figure 2-11. Creating a new activity

To get started defining this application's activities, right click on the project, click on Add→New Item, select Mono for Android→Activity, and name it *FirstActivity.cs* (see Figure 2-11). There will be some sample code generated in the activity, but you can replace it with the code from Example 2-13.

Example 2-13. FirstActivity.cs

```
using System;
using Android.App;
using Android.Content;
using Android.OS;
using Android.Widget;

namespace Chapter2.MonoAndroidApp
{
    [Activity(Label = "Hello, Android!", MainLauncher = true, Icon = "@drawable/icon")] ❶
    public class FirstActivity : Activity
    {
        protected override void OnCreate(Bundle bundle) ❷
        {
            base.OnCreate(bundle);

            SetContentView(Resource.Layout.First); ❸

            var button = FindViewById<Button>(Resource.Id.Button); ❹
            button.Click += buttonClicked; ❺
        }
```

```
        private void buttonClicked(object sender, EventArgs e)
        {
            var intent = new Intent(this, typeof (SecondActivity)); ❻
            intent.PutExtra("text", DateTime.Now.ToLongTimeString()); ❼

            StartActivity(intent); ❽
        }
    }
}
```

❶ Decorate the class with `ActivityAttribute` to let the Android runtime know that this is one of our activities.

❷ The activity lifecycle has many different events you can hook into depending on what you want to do. More often than not, the first entry point you want in its lifecycle is `OnCreate()`, which we'll use here.

❸ The first thing we do is call `SetContentView()`, passing in the ID constant for the layout to use for this activity. This will load up and inflate the layout in that file, allowing you to access any elements inside of it with an identifier.

❹ Use the `FindViewById()` method, passing in the ID of the button, to get a reference to the button in the layout. The generic version used here will cast the view object to a `Button` for you, a shortcut to help clean up the code and make it a little more readable.

❺ Assign a handler method for the button's `click` event.

❻ When the button is clicked, create a new intent, setting its type to the class `SecondActivity` (which will be created next).

❼ In order to pass values along with the intent, they can be added as "extras." For this message, add a string extra with the key "text," assigning the value to a string representing the current time.

❽ Now that the intent is ready, inform Android that we want to start this activity by passing it into the `StartActivity()` method.

Let's take a closer look at what's going on with the `ActivityAttribute` used to decorate the class. All components in your application must be registered in the application's *AndroidManifest.xml* file. If you forget to register the component, your application will crash, since Android won't know about it. To simplify things, Mono for Android provides attributes like this one that will generate that XML for you at compile time. There are many options you can set through the attribute, but let's run through the ones used here:

MainLauncher

Since an application can have many activities, this property allows you to specify which activities should be entry points into the application. These activities are what will show up in the device's list of applications.

Label

> This is the text label used along with the activity's icon in the launcher, and is also shown in the activity's title bar by default.

Icon

> This drawable resource is used as this activity's icon when displayed in the device's list of applications.

Finally, we need to create the activity for the second screen of the application. Add a new activity to the project named SecondActivity. This uses the layout defined for the second screen, *Second.axml*, and sets the label's text to the value passed in through the intent created in FirstActivity (see Example 2-14):

Example 2-14. SecondActivity.cs

```
using Android.App;
using Android.OS;
using Android.Widget;

namespace Chapter2.MonoAndroidApp
{
    [Activity(Label = "Second Activity")]
    public class SecondActivity : Activity
    {
        protected override void OnCreate(Bundle savedInstanceState)
        {
            base.OnCreate(savedInstanceState);

            SetContentView(Resource.Layout.Second); ❶

            var text = FindViewById<TextView>(Resource.Id.Text); ❷
            text.Text = Intent.GetStringExtra("text"); ❸
        }
    }
}
```

❶ Use the layout from *Second.axml* for this activity.

❷ Find the TextView we want to update inside the layout.

❸ The Intent property provided by the base class here provides access to the Intent used to launch this activity. Using the same key used to load the string into the intent, use the GetStringExtra() method on the intent to pull it back out and assign it to the TextView's Text property.

That's everything needed for this application, so it's time to run it! Select Debug→Start Without Debugging to launch the application. This should pull up the "Select Device" dialog, which is most likely empty, since this is the first time we're launching the application. Click on "Start emulator image" and start one of the emulator images available to use. For more information on how to create new emulator images, refer to Appendix A.

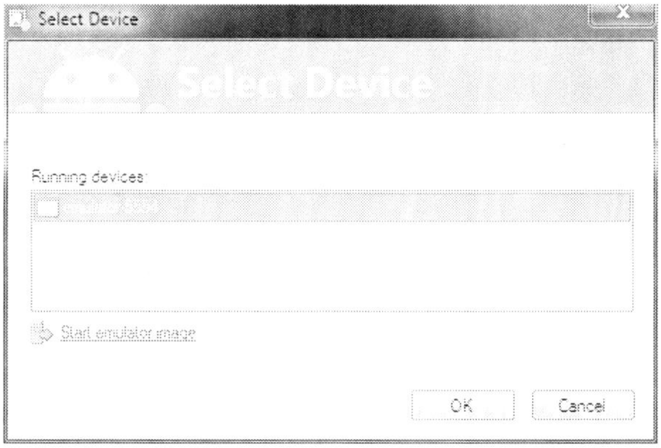

Figure 2-12. Selecting a device to deploy to

Once the emulator finishes launching, select it in the list of running devices (see Figure 2-12), and Mono for Android will deploy your application to the emulator. This can take a little while the first time, as it installs the debug runtime, but subsequent deployments will be much faster. Once the application starts up, it should look like Figure 2-13. Congratulations—you have just built your first Android application!

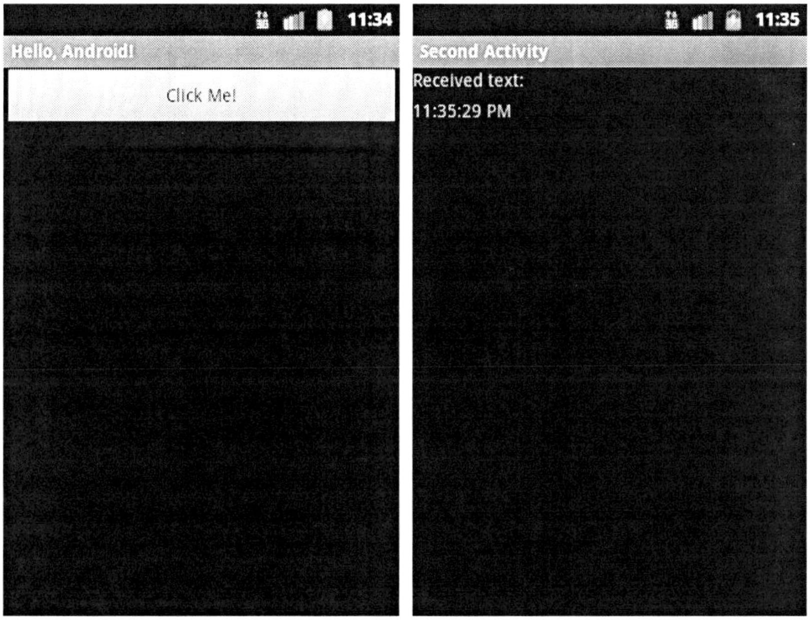

Figure 2-13. Running the application in the emulator

Windows Phone

Now that the iOS and Android applications are up and running, that brings us to Windows Phone. In order to develop for the Windows Phone platform, you must be running either Windows Vista or Windows 7. While there are numerous steps to getting started on the other platforms (even though Xamarin simplifies this somewhat with their chain installers) getting started with Windows Phone requires much less effort. In order to begin, you must download the Windows Phone SDK, which can be found at *create.msdn.com*. The SDK installer includes all of the tools you need to get started, including the IDE. If you already have Visual Studio 2010 installed on your computer, you will be able to continue using that, but in case you don't, the installer also includes the free Visual Studio 2010 Express for Windows Phone. The Windows Phone emulator is also included in the install, as well as various other packages to help out with development.

 There have been multiple releases of both the Windows Phone SDK and versions of the operating system. This book is going to assume that you have downloaded and installed version 7.1 or later of the Windows Phone SDK, which includes support for both Windows Phone 7 and Windows Phone 7.5, codenamed Mango. The Mango release included many new features, some of which we'll touch on later in this book.

There are two main development paths for Windows Phone applications: Silverlight and XNA. XNA is essentially focused on game development, and is also found on other platforms such as Windows, Zune, and Xbox 360. For the purposes of this book, we are going to focus entirely on the Silverlight side of Windows Phone development.

Create the Application

With both iOS and Android, there was a layer provided by the Mono tools to bridge the native platforms and the .NET framework, but since .NET is the native framework on Windows Phone, that's not something you need to worry about here. In Visual Studio, create a new solution by clicking File→New Project. Choose Silverlight for Windows Phone→Windows Phone Application and name it Chapter2.WindowsPhoneApp (see Figure 2-14). When prompted about which platform version you would like to target, select Windows Phone OS 7.1.

In the New Project dialog, you might notice some terms you might not recognize. These are part of the Windows Phone design language named Metro: *pivot* and *panorama*. A pivot view roughly translates to what would be a tabbed view in iOS or Android. Along the top of the view are headers for each pivot item and you can swipe left and right to switch between them (see Figure 2-15). In the emulator, you can look at the Settings application for an example of a pivot view.

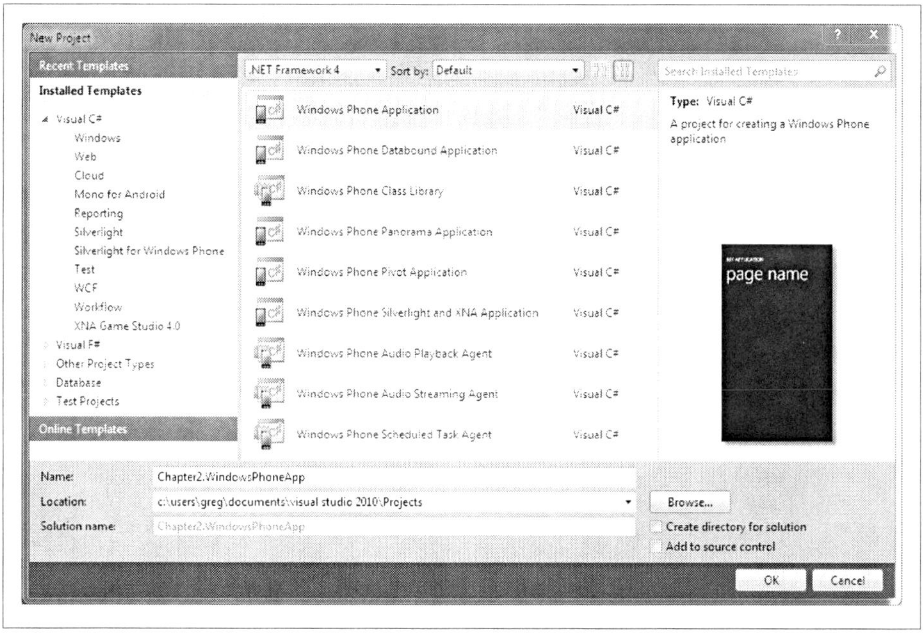

Figure 2-14. Create a new application

The panorama view has similar interaction metaphors to the pivot view but typically represents a single space much larger than the screen, encouraging the user to explore by showing hints of what lies just off the edge of the screen (see Figure 2-16). For this application, you will be using a simple single-page layout, but as you start building richer applications, the pivot and panorama views become very useful for defining your interface and remaining consistent with other applications on the platform.

Once you create the new project, you should now see a fresh Windows Phone solution that contains various files, including:

App.xaml
> A class that manages the overall lifecycle of the application

ApplicationIcon.png
> The icon shown next to the application in the phone's application list

Background.png
> The tile background when the application is pinned to the phone's home screen as a live tile

MainPage.xaml
> The default starting page to show in the application when it launches

SplashScreenImage.jpg
> The image shown to the user while the user is waiting for the application to start

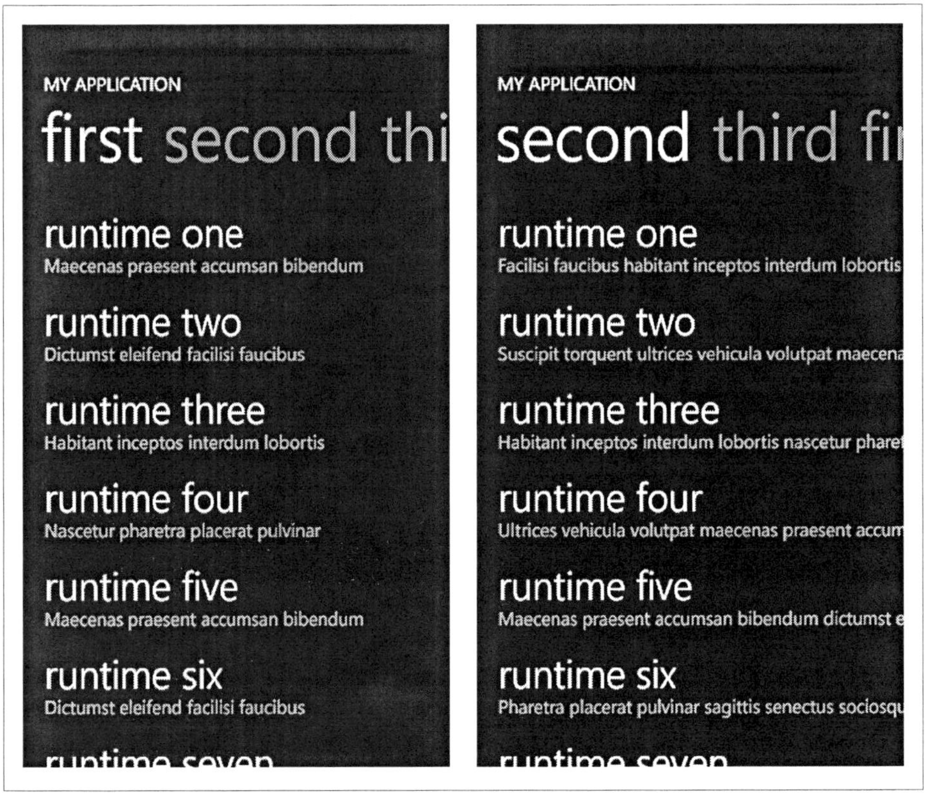

Figure 2-15. A Windows Phone pivot application

Properties→WMAppManifest.xml

> The manifest contains configuration details about the application, such as the list of capabilities used

If you open up the project's properties in the Application tab (see Figure 2-17), you'll find some basic application settings, such as the application's title and the name for the *XAP* file (the package you use to distribute and install the application).

For this simple application, you can leave most of the default project template alone. However, before we start customizing, let's take a quick look at *WMAppManifest.xml*, located in the *Properties* folder. This file contains many configuration details about the application. Inside you'll find a list of capabilities to make available to the application, as well as the default starting page of your application (see Example 2-15 for a trimmed down version) in case you want to change it from the default of *MainPage.xaml*.

Figure 2-16. A Windows Phone panorama application

Example 2-15. WMAppManifest.xml (simplified)

```xml
<?xml version="1.0" encoding="utf-8"?>
<Deployment>
  <App>
    <IconPath IsRelative="true" IsResource="false">ApplicationIcon.png</IconPath>
    <Capabilities>
      <Capability Name="ID_CAP_LOCATION"/>
    </Capabilities>
    <Tasks>
      <DefaultTask  Name ="_default" NavigationPage="MainPage.xaml"/>
    </Tasks>
  </App>
</Deployment>
```

Windows Phone applications are essentially made up of a series of *pages* that you can navigate between to form the flow of the application. The definition of pages in Windows Phone applications is very similar to how they are defined on the web. Pages can link to other pages in order to expose other pieces of the application, and the new page is pushed onto the top of the navigation stack. All Windows Phone devices provide a

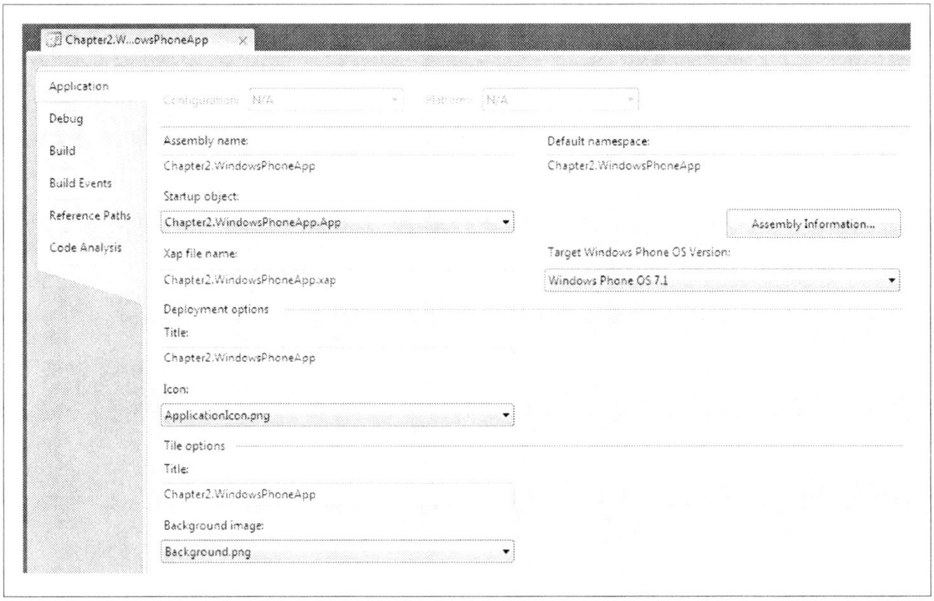

Figure 2-17. Windows Phone Application options

hardware Back button which will pop the current page off the top of the stack, navigating back to the previous page on the navigation stack, just like a web browser would.

To navigate to a new page, you use a *Uniform Resource Identifier (URI)* that provides the path to the page's file within the application. Optionally, you can pass extra data into the page by including it in the URI's *query string*, much like you would in programming for the web. For example, consider the following page URI:

```
/MainPage.xaml?year=2012&name=Greg
```

Navigating to this URI will load up the *MainPage.xaml* page, passing in two parameters through the query string, `year` and `name`. If this page is loaded again later on, such as when the user hits the back button to navigate back to this page, the same parameters sent through the query string will be provided to the page. This allows it to pick up where it left off.

Defining the Interface

Open up *MainPage.xaml*, which is the starting point for the application, as specified in *WMAppManifest.xaml*. When you first load up the file, the default view is most likely split between the designer and *XAML* panels. XAML is a declarative markup language found used in .NET frameworks such as Silverlight and WPF to create user interfaces. XAML itself is a very deep and powerful markup language that we will only scratch the surface of in this book, so I highly recommend doing some more reading on it in order to dig into that power as you need it.

As you would expect with any designer surface, you have the option of dragging user interface elements from Visual Studio's toolbox onto the surface to add and modify them. However, in order to start getting a feel of what XAML markup is like, we'll create this application's simple markup by hand. For this simple layout, there isn't much that needs to change from the default markup filled in by the template (see Example 2-16).

Example 2-16. MainPage.xaml

```
<phone:PhoneApplicationPage ❶
    x:Class="Chapter2.WindowsPhoneApp.MainPage"
    xmlns="http://schemas.microsoft.com/winfx/2006/xaml/presentation"
    xmlns:x="http://schemas.microsoft.com/winfx/2006/xaml"
    xmlns:phone="clr-namespace:Microsoft.Phone.Controls;assembly=Microsoft.Phone"
    xmlns:shell="clr-namespace:Microsoft.Phone.Shell;assembly=Microsoft.Phone"
    xmlns:d="http://schemas.microsoft.com/expression/blend/2008"
    xmlns:mc="http://schemas.openxmlformats.org/markup-compatibility/2006"
    mc:Ignorable="d" d:DesignWidth="480" d:DesignHeight="768"
    FontFamily="{StaticResource PhoneFontFamilyNormal}"
    FontSize="{StaticResource PhoneFontSizeNormal}"
    Foreground="{StaticResource PhoneForegroundBrush}"
    SupportedOrientations="Portrait" Orientation="Portrait"
    shell:SystemTray.IsVisible="True">

    <Grid x:Name="LayoutRoot" Background="Transparent"> ❷
        <Grid.RowDefinitions>
            <RowDefinition Height="Auto"/>
            <RowDefinition Height="*"/>
        </Grid.RowDefinitions>

        <StackPanel x:Name="TitlePanel" Grid.Row="0" Margin="12,17,0,28"> ❸
            <TextBlock x:Name="ApplicationTitle" Text="Hello, Windows Phone 7!"
Style="{StaticResource PhoneTextNormalStyle}"/>
            <TextBlock x:Name="PageTitle" Text="first page" Margin="9,-7,0,0"
Style="{StaticResource PhoneTextTitle1Style}"/>
        </StackPanel>

        <StackPanel x:Name="ContentPanel" Grid.Row="1" Margin="12,0,12,0"> ❹
            <Button x:Name="Button" Content="Click Me!" Height="100" Click="ButtonClicked" /
> ❺
        </StackPanel>
    </Grid>

</phone:PhoneApplicationPage>
```

❶ Each page in an application derives from the class PhoneApplicationPage. Attributes of this element define namespaces and other options which you can ignore for now, leaving all of the defaults in place.

❷ For the root layout element of the page we'll use a Grid, which functions much like a table. Define two rows for the table, which will be filled in next.

❸ The first grid row represents the title bar of the page, a common feature in Windows Phone pages. The title bar for this page will display the application name, and then the page name in larger text below it. A StackPanel is a simple layout container which, much like LinearLayout in Android, will stack child elements either horizontally or vertically.

❹ For the second grid row define another StackPanel, this one containing just the Button element.

❺ In the button's attributes, declare that a method named ButtonClicked will handle the event fired when the button is clicked. This method does not yet exist, but will be created later.

That takes care of the layout for the first page, so let's move on to building the layout for the second page. Right click on the solution and click Add→New Item. Select Windows Phone Portrait Page, and name it *SecondPage.xaml* (see Figure 2-18). This should create a new page that looks just like *MainPage.xaml* did before we modified it. Now we will tweak the markup for this new page to be very similar to the first page, but instead of the button it will display the text sent into it, as shown in Example 2-17.

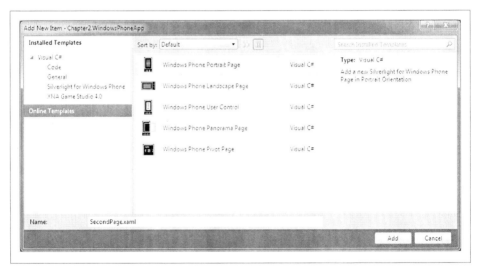

Figure 2-18. Add a new page to the application

Example 2-17. SecondPage.xaml

```
<phone:PhoneApplicationPage
    x:Class="Chapter2.WindowsPhoneApp.SecondPage"
    xmlns="http://schemas.microsoft.com/winfx/2006/xaml/presentation"
    xmlns:x="http://schemas.microsoft.com/winfx/2006/xaml"
    xmlns:phone="clr-namespace:Microsoft.Phone.Controls;assembly=Microsoft.Phone"
    xmlns:shell="clr-namespace:Microsoft.Phone.Shell;assembly=Microsoft.Phone"
    xmlns:d="http://schemas.microsoft.com/expression/blend/2008"
    xmlns:mc="http://schemas.openxmlformats.org/markup-compatibility/2006"
```

```
        FontFamily="{StaticResource PhoneFontFamilyNormal}"
        FontSize="{StaticResource PhoneFontSizeNormal}"
        Foreground="{StaticResource PhoneForegroundBrush}"
        SupportedOrientations="Portrait" Orientation="Portrait"
        mc:Ignorable="d" d:DesignHeight="768" d:DesignWidth="480"
        shell:SystemTray.IsVisible="True">

    <Grid x:Name="LayoutRoot" Background="Transparent">
        <Grid.RowDefinitions>
            <RowDefinition Height="Auto"/>
            <RowDefinition Height="*"/>
        </Grid.RowDefinitions>

        <StackPanel x:Name="TitlePanel" Grid.Row="0" Margin="12,17,0,28"> ❶
            <TextBlock x:Name="ApplicationTitle" Text="Hello, Windows Phone 7!"
Style="{StaticResource PhoneTextNormalStyle}"/>
            <TextBlock x:Name="PageTitle" Text="second page" Margin="9,-7,0,0"
Style="{StaticResource PhoneTextTitle1Style}"/>
        </StackPanel>

        <StackPanel x:Name="ContentPanel" Grid.Row="1" Margin="12,0,12,0">
            <TextBlock Text="Received text:" /> ❷
            <TextBlock x:Name="TextReceived" /> ❸
        </StackPanel>
    </Grid>

</phone:PhoneApplicationPage>
```

❶ Use the same title panel format from `MainPage.xaml`, updating the page title to say "second page".

❷ Create a label using a `TextBlock` element.

❸ Use another `TextBlock` element to display the text received from the first page, assigning it an ID so it can be referenced from code.

Writing the Application Code

That takes care of the layout, so now it's time to wire up the views. First, open up *MainPage.xaml.cs* by right-clicking *MainPage.xaml* and selecting View Code or by expanding it in the Solution Explorer. This is the code side of the class defined in XAML, commonly referred to as the *code-behind*. If you recall from the XAML for this page we declared that the button used a click handler method named `ButtonClicked`, so this method needs to be added to the code-behind, as shown in Example 2-18.

Example 2-18. MainPage.xaml.cs

```
using System;
using System.Net;
using System.Windows;
using Microsoft.Phone.Controls;

namespace Chapter2.WindowsPhoneApp
{
```

```
public partial class MainPage : PhoneApplicationPage
{
    public MainPage()
    {
        InitializeComponent();
    }

    private void ButtonClicked(object sender, RoutedEventArgs e) ❶
    {
        NavigationService.Navigate( ❷
            new Uri("/SecondPage.xaml?text=" +
                    HttpUtility.UrlEncode(DateTime.Now.ToLongTimeString()),
                    UriKind.Relative));
    }
}
}
```

❶ Define `ButtonClicked` as a private method of the class. Since `MainPage` is declared as a partial class, the XAML and code-behind sides are all part of the same underlying class, defined across multiple files.

❷ When the button is clicked, we tell the operating system to navigate to a new page, passing data into the new page using the query string. The use of the `UrlEncode` method here is very important. When passing data into another page during navigation, make sure you properly encode any query string parameters in order to make sure they make it into the next page correctly.

 A very popular design pattern for building Windows Phone applications is *Model-View-ViewModel (MVVM)*, which minimizes the amount of code you place in code-behind files by allowing you to take full advantage of the power of XAML. MVVM is a topic all of its own, so the examples in this book will stick to using the code-behind files to stay focused on the core concepts and keep things as simple as possible.

Finally, open up *SecondPage.xaml.cs*, the code-behind file for *SecondPage.xaml*. The lifecycle of a page in Windows Phone has many events you can hook into. For this page, we want to extract a value from the query string when loading the page and update the UI accordingly. To accomplish this we will tap into the `OnNavigatedTo` method (see Example 2-19):

Example 2-19. SecondPage.xaml.cs

```
using Microsoft.Phone.Controls;

namespace Chapter2.WindowsPhoneApp
{
    public partial class SecondPage : PhoneApplicationPage
    {
        public SecondPage()
        {
```

```
        InitializeComponent();
    }

    protected override void OnNavigatedTo(System.Windows.Navigation.NavigationEventArgs
e) ❶
    {
        base.OnNavigatedTo(e);

        TextReceived.Text = NavigationContext.QueryString["text"]; ❷
    }
  }
}
```

❶ The `OnNavigatedTo` method is called when this page transitions into being the active page in the window, including when it is loaded from cache.

❷ The query string can be accessed through the `NavigationContext.QueryString` property, so use that to retrieve the value and display it in the UI.

That's all the code you need for this application, so now you can fire it up in the emulator by pressing F5 or starting it from the Debug menu in Visual Studio. This will start the emulator if it is not already running, deploy the application and then launch it. If all went according to plan, your application should look like Figure 2-19. You are now a Windows Phone developer!

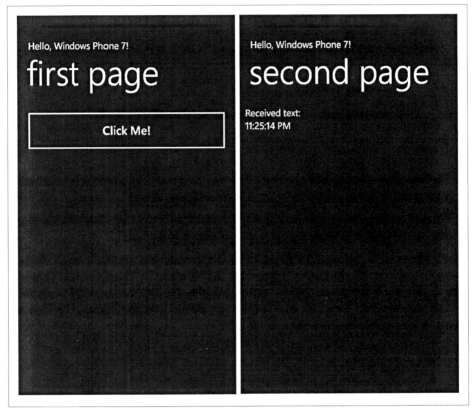

Figure 2-19. Running the application in the emulator

Summary

In this chapter, we walked through the process of creating simple applications for iOS, Android, and Windows Phone. For each of them we touched on how to set up your environments and create a new project, as well as exploring the basic building blocks available to build applications on them. For iOS and Android, we also looked at what MonoTouch and Mono for Android provide and how they interact with the native platform to allow you to write native applications while taking advantage of the .NET Framework. We have only scratched the surface of what each platform has to offer, but hopefully you're starting to get a feel for how to work with each of them. As you build out more applications in later chapters, things should start to feel more familiar. In the next chapter, we will start to explore various techniques for sharing code across all three platforms.

CHAPTER 3

Code Sharing Techniques

In the last chapter, you built simple applications for iOS, Android, and Windows Phone. Even though each provided identical functionality, they were implemented completely independently of one another. This works fine for a simple application with one button and two screens, but is certainly not ideal for real world applications.

As mentioned in Chapter 1, one major benefit of the .NET approach is being able to share a lot of your non-UI code across all platforms. At first, you might think that almost all behavior in most applications is tied to the user interface in one way or another, which would make it very difficult to share any code across platforms. While this may seem true at a higher level, if you dig a little deeper, you'll find it is often not the case.

For example, consider an application that accesses a web service to download its data in XML format, and then transforms that XML into some model classes that the application can use. All of this code is actually independent of the presentation layer and can therefore be shared across each platform (see Figure 3-1). You only need to write the code for the web service client, XML processing and model classes once, but get to reuse them everywhere.

It's easy to see how this can apply to many other classes of functionality as well, such as libraries that perform calculations, process data, and process data. In many cases, you will find that the code that can be shared is often the real core of the application, which is often the hardest part to get right in the first place. With this approach, you only need to get that part right once to know that it will be useful everywhere.

This chapter will walk through setting up a shared class library and then explore several techniques you can apply to get as much code reuse as possible.

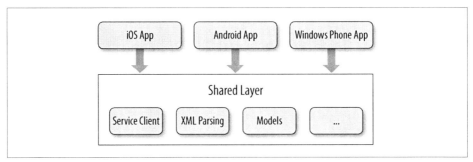

Figure 3-1. An example of a shared architecture

Project Setup

When working with code you want to share across multiple platforms, you'll want to keep it in separate class library projects that get referenced by your applications. The examples in this chapter and throughout the rest of the book will build up a class library project named `SharedLibrary` that contains all shared cross-platform code.

Create a folder named *SharedLibrary*, which will contain the shared library projects. Since developing for all three platforms requires both Windows and Mac OS X, these instructions will assume you put this folder somewhere that can be accessed by both systems, such as a file share, source control, or some other means. If you are limited to just one operating system, you can simply skip the steps for that platform and move on to the others.

Open up either Visual Studio or MonoDevelop, depending on your system, and create a new .NET class library named `SharedLibrary` inside of that *SharedLibrary* folder. Note that this should be a standard .NET class library (C#→Library in MonoDevelop or Windows→Class Library in Visual Studio) and not one specific to one of the mobile platforms. Remove any classes that might have been added by default in the project template so that the project is empty.

Next, you'll need to create separate class library projects for each platform, also putting each of them in the *SharedLibrary* folder. If you're wondering why you need to create all of these projects, this will make more sense after the next section on file linking. In MonoDevelop on your Mac, start by creating a new solution, select Mono-Touch→MonoTouch Library Project, and name it `SharedLibrary.MonoTouch`. Again, re-move any files added automatically by the template. Right click on the solution and click on Add→Add Existing Project. In the dialog it opens, select *SharedLibrary/SharedLibrary.csproj*, the .NET class library created before.

Following the same procedure as with MonoTouch, create a new class library for Android by selecting Mono for Android→Mono for Android Library Project, naming it `SharedLibrary.MonoAndroid`. This can be done with either MonoDevelop or Visual

Studio, depending on your environment. As before, remove any default classes and add the existing SharedLibrary project to the solution.

Finally, create a new solution in Visual Studio on Windows, selecting Silverlight for Windows Phone→Windows Phone Class Library and naming it SharedLibrary.WindowsPhone. Just like the first two projects, remove any classes added automatically and add the SharedLibrary project to the solution.

 By default, when a solution only has one project in it, Visual Studio's solution explorer will only show the project and not the solution. This can make it difficult to add new projects to the solution quickly. In Visual Studio's options, under Projects and Solutions→General, there is a checkbox labeled "Always show solution" which will make Visual Studio show the solution in the explorer regardless of how many projects there are.

With these projects set up, it's time to start looking at code-sharing techniques. Imagine that you are tasked with building an application that lets a user save her current location when she parks her car, and then provide her with a notification once she returns within a certain proximity of that spot. While the following examples won't build out the entire application, they will focus on how you might apply these techniques to writing the core logic of the application.

File Linking

In the last section, you created separate class libraries for each platform, which might seem counterproductive to sharing code. The problem is that you cannot simply take a DLL compiled for the full .NET framework, reference it in a project targeting a different platform, and expect it to run flawlessly. While it's possible that this would actually work, it comes with an unnecessary level of risk. Each platform defines its own *profile* that it exposes, which specifies which areas of .NET it includes.

 The reason for the differences between profiles is that many times there are parts of the framework that may not make sense everywhere. For example, the System.Configuration namespace is found in the full .NET Framework, and is used for handling configuration data for desktop and web applications. However, this namespace is intentionally absent from the Windows Phone and mobile Mono profiles, as it doesn't apply to those frameworks.

If the DLL uses a method present in the full .NET framework profile but absent from the target platform, your application will crash when it tries to invoke that method. This is a risk present in using a compiled DLL on any platform other the one it was compiled for, such as using a .NET class library DLL in a Silverlight application, so this problem is not limited to mobile applications.

By compiling the code through these separate projects, you end up with a version of the library compiled specifically against each platform. This allows you to be certain at compile time that you are not referencing an unsupported piece of the framework for a given platform. To share source code across each platform, you can create separate copies of each file for each project, but that would quickly turn into a maintainability nightmare in trying to keep the copies in sync with each other.

Thankfully it's possible, through what is called *file linking*, to maintain a single copy of the file and still compile it across different projects. File linking is a feature supported in both Visual Studio and MonoDevelop. When you link a file to a project, it will be treated as if it were a part of that project, but the actual file will still only live in its original location. This allows you to edit the file in one place and have it take effect everywhere that references it. One thing to keep in mind is that linking is done on a per-file basis, so projects can contain a mixture of both linked and local source files.

In the case of our library, the main `SharedLibrary` project will serve as the "source" containing the actual files, which will be linked into the different class libraries created for iOS, Android, and Windows Phone. Start out by creating a new folder named *Chapter3* in that project and adding a new class named `ParkingSpotTracker` to it. This class will be built up later, but for now you can leave it empty.

Open up the `SharedProject.MonoTouch` solution and create the *Chapter3* folder in there as well. Right-click on that folder, click on Add→Add Files, and select *ParkingSpot-Tracker.cs* from the source library project. MonoDevelop will prompt you to specify how you would like the file added to the project (see Figure 3-2). From the list of options, select "Add a link to the file" and then click OK to add the linked file to the project. MonoDevelop also provides the ability to add a link to an entire folder in order to process many files at once by selecting Add→Add Existing Folder. This simply adds them in bulk, and will not monitor the folder for changes after the fact.

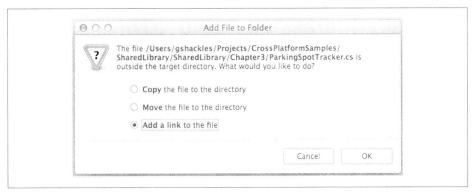

Figure 3-2. Adding a linked file in MonoDevelop

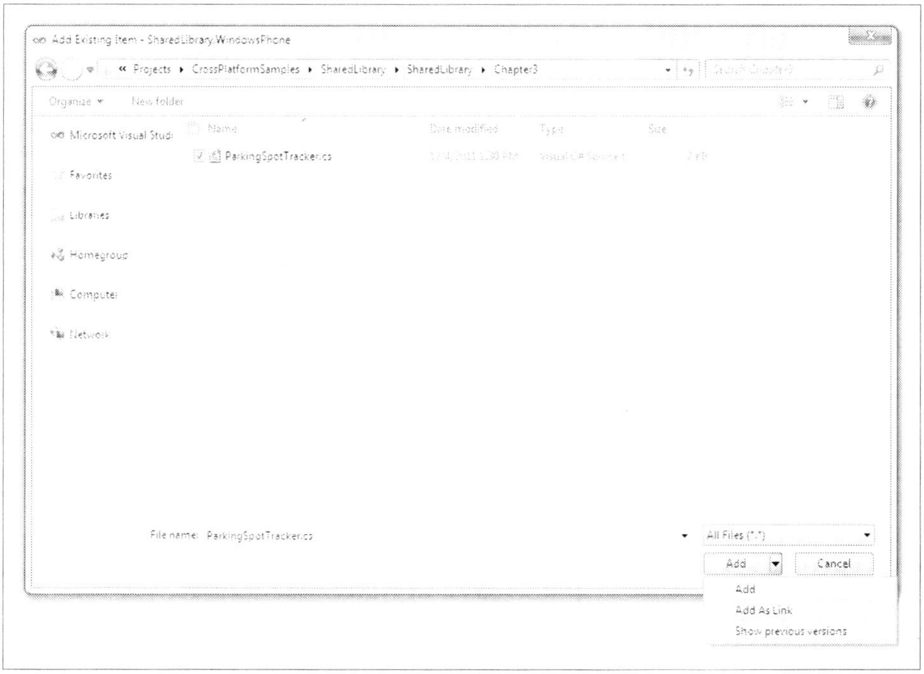

![Add Existing Item dialog box in Visual Studio 2010 showing the ParkingSpotTracker.cs file with an Add button and Add As Link option expanded.]

Figure 3-3. Adding a linked file in Visual Studio 2010

Next, open the `SharedProject.WindowsPhone` solution in Visual Studio and create the *Chapter3* folder. Right-click on the folder, click Add→Existing Item and select *ParkingSpotTracker.cs* from the source library project. Before clicking the Add button, click on the arrow on its right side and select Add As Link (see Figure 3-3). This will add the file to the project as a link the same way MonoDevelop did. Go ahead and repeat this process with the `SharedProject.MonoAndroid` solution using either Visual Studio or MonoDevelop.

The process of creating and managing linked files across projects can be tedious but is certainly worth the effort. If you're using Visual Studio 2010, you can download the Project Linker extension, developed by Microsoft, which helps make this even easier. With this extension, you can specify projects you want linked, and it will watch the source project for updates and create or remove the linked files for you automatically. More information about this extension is available at *http://msdn.micro soft.com/en-us/library/ff921108*

Abstraction

Despite the fact that each platform operates in its own way, there is still some commonality that exists between them. For example, each platform's API exposes a way to ask the device for its current location. The code to accomplish this is different for each of them, meaning it cannot be shared, but the end result is the same. In most cases, your business layer won't necessarily care *how* the data is obtained; it just wants to know what that data is. By abstracting out the implementation from the definition, the shared layer can still make use of the results of these features without having to know anything about how they are implemented.

In C#, this typically means creating an *interface*. An interface is similar to a class definition, except that it only contains the signatures for its properties and methods rather than including the implementation as well. Any class that implements an interface must provide implementations for everything defined in that interface. A single class can also implement multiple interfaces.

Since an interface only contains the definitions, it forms a contract between the client and the implementation. The shared layer can work against that contract without needing to be tied to a particular implementation, and each platform's application can then provide its own implementation of that contract. This allows for a better separation of concerns, keeping the core application logic in one shared place, decoupled from platform specifics.

For the parking spot tracking application, the geolocation functionality is what will be abstracted away from the shared layer. In the *Chapter3* folder of `SharedLibrary`, add a new class named `LocationInfo` (see Example 3-1) that will store latitude and longitude information for a specific point on a map. It also includes a method for calculating the distance between it and another point, which will return a fake value for this example. Next, define an interface named `ILocationProvider` that contains a single method, `GetCurrentLocation()`, which returns a `LocationInfo` object representing the user's current location (see Example 3-2). This is the geolocation contract for the application. Finally, modify *ParkingSpotTracker.cs* to require an implementation of `ILocationProvider` be given to it, and then add a method named `ParkHere()` that checks the current location (see Example 3-3).

Example 3-1. LocationInfo.cs

```
namespace SharedLibrary.Chapter3
{
    public class LocationInfo
    {
        public double Latitude { get; private set; }
        public double Longitude { get; private set; }

        public LocationInfo (double latitude, double longitude)
        {
            Latitude = latitude;
```

```
                Longitude = longitude;
        }

        public double DistanceInMetersFrom(LocationInfo point)
        {
            return 42;
        }
    }
}
```

Example 3-2. ILocationProvider.cs

```
namespace SharedLibrary.Chapter3
{
    public interface ILocationProvider
    {
        LocationInfo GetCurrentLocation();
    }
}
```

Example 3-3. ParkingSpotTracker.cs

```
using System;

namespace SharedLibrary.Chapter3
{
    public class ParkingSpotTracker
    {
        private readonly ILocationProvider _locationProvider;

        public ParkingSpotTracker(ILocationProvider locationProvider) ❶
        {
            _locationProvider = locationProvider;
        }

        public void ParkHere() ❷
        {
            var currentLocation = _locationProvider.GetCurrentLocation();

            // save a new parking spot using currentLocation
        }
    }
}
```

❶ Require that an implementation of ILocationProvider be passed into this class.

❷ Add a method named ParkHere() that reads in the user's current location and then, in a real implementation, saves it somewhere.

Abstraction can be a very powerful way to separate your core business logic from a particular platform's implementation, and is not limited to sharing code across mobile platforms. When applied correctly, it will result in a codebase that, in addition to being easier to share across platforms, is also much easier to test and maintain.

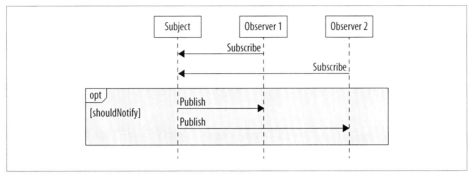

Figure 3-4. Publishing an event to multiple subscribers

Following the methods described in the last section, link these new files into the iOS, Android, and Windows Phone class libraries. We will explore more complete examples of the abstraction pattern later in this book, when working with the location and data persistence APIs.

Observer Pattern

When designing your application, you might run into situations where you want the application to be able to react to something happening in the shared layer. However, since the shared layer is intentionally ignorant of any specific platform, making a direct connection here can be difficult. One option would be to use the abstraction pattern and abstract out everything in the user interface you might use, such as showing an alert message or a progress indicator. That is generally not a good idea when working with any user interface functionality, since it starts to force the same interface paradigms on all platforms and defeats the entire purpose of this approach to cross-platform development. Why should the Windows Phone application have to show an alert just because the Android application does? Forcing this requirement will lead to business logic that is tightly coupled to the user interface. A pattern that is especially useful in decoupling business logic from the user interface is the *observer pattern*.

The observer pattern is a messaging pattern in which an object, the *subject*, can publish updates about what it's doing. Other objects, the *observers*, can subscribe to these updates and receive notifications when they occur (see Figure 3-4). In this model, the subject can publish these updates when it needs to without having to worry about whether or not there are any observers watching for them. This pattern is commonly found in UI frameworks where you can subscribe to actions happening in the interface, such as a button being clicked, but it can be applied in the other direction as well.

In .NET, the observer pattern is built right into the framework in its implementation of *events*. Using the terms defined by the observer pattern, a .NET event is the message published by the subject. When the event is defined, it also declares its *delegate*, which specifies what data is sent to observers of the event when it occurs. You can create your own delegate signature according to your needs, but the .NET Framework also provides the built-in EventHandler delegate that will often do what you need, saving you from having to declare a delegate manually for every event. The next example will demonstrate how you can use this approach to define an event that sends back specialized data to its observers.

For the parking spot tracking application, one of the feature requirements is that it will poll the current location occasionally, checking to see if it is within range of the stored parking spot location. When a nearby spot is found, the application needs a way to be notified so it can inform the user. To implement this, define an event on the ParkingSpotTracker class that the application can subscribe to. Start by creating a class named SpotDetectedNearbyEventArgs (see Example 3-4), an object containing the distance between the user and the parking spot. This object will be sent back to the subscriber when the event is fired. Creating a custom class for event arguments is not necessary, but can be useful for relaying any extra information along with the event (see Example 3-5).

Example 3-4. SpotDetectedNearbyEventArgs.cs

```
using System;

namespace SharedLibrary.Chapter3
{
    public class SpotDetectedNearbyEventArgs : EventArgs
    {
        public double Distance { get; private set; }

        public SpotDetectedNearbyEventArgs(double distance)
        {
            Distance = distance;
        }
    }
}
```

Example 3-5. ParkingSpotTracker.cs (updates only)

```
using System;

namespace SharedLibrary.Chapter3
{
    public class ParkingSpotTracker
    {
        // only including updated parts to this class

        public event EventHandler<SpotDetectedNearbyEventArgs> SpotDetectedNearby; ❶

        private void checkCurrentLocation() ❷
        {
            var currentLocation = _locationProvider.GetCurrentLocation(); ❸
            var newYorkCity = new LocationInfo(40.716667, -74); ❹

            double distance = currentLocation.DistanceInMetersFrom(newYorkCity); ❺
```

```
            if (distance < 100 && SpotDetectedNearby != null)
            {
                SpotDetectedNearby(this, new SpotDetectedNearbyEventArgs(distance)); ❻
            }
        }
    }
}
```

❶ Define the SpotDetectedNearby event using the SpotDetectedNearbyEventArgs class.

❷ Add a method named checkCurrentLocation() that, in a real implementation, would be called periodically.

❸ Ask the location provider for the user's current location.

❹ For demo purposes, pretend that the user had parked at the coordinates for New York City.

❺ Calculate the distance between the user and New York City.

❻ If the user is within 100 meters, and there are event subscribers, fire the event.

By implementing the nearby spot notification as an event, the business layer remains completely independent of the user interface layer. Each platform's application is free to process the event however it wants, giving it full freedom to behave like other native apps on the platform.

Partial Classes

Earlier in this chapter, you saw that the abstraction pattern can be useful in catering to platform differences while still getting a lot of code reuse. However, in cases where most of a class can be shared across platforms and you simply want to provide some extensions for specific platforms, abstraction can sometimes become cumbersome. In these scenarios, C#'s support for *partial classes* can be very useful. Partial classes allow you to split the definition of a class across multiple files. These files will be merged at compile time and treated as though they were in the same file.

Partial classes are commonly found in platforms that make use of generated source code, such as ASP.NET Web Forms and Windows Forms. By using partial classes, the developer can work in an entirely separate file from the generated code, avoiding any collision between them but still providing a single class implementation to the compiler. This approach is also used by MonoTouch's view controller designer files and Mono for Android's resource classes.

The usefulness of partial classes is not limited to cases involving generated code. When combined with file linking, partial classes allow you to share the common source across each platform, but then also augment that with platform-specific extensions as needed. Since the different files are seen as one logical file in the eyes of the compiler, each part has full access to anything defined in the others, including private variables and methods. This is a very powerful technique, but overuse of it can lead to code that is difficult to follow, since it may not be obvious where all pieces of a class are.

To demonstrate this approach, let's say that on Android you want to extend the ParkingSpotTracker class with a method that honks the user's car horn. For the sake of this example, assume that this is a feature specific to Android, and is not available on other platforms. First, add the partial keyword to the class definition to specify that you want to allow the class to be defined across multiple parts (see Example 3-6). All parts of this class must also be declared in the same way. In addition, you must take care to define them within the same namespace, since classes with the same name in different namespaces are effectively separate classes.

Example 3-6. ParkingSpotTracker.cs (updates only)

```
using System;

namespace SharedLibrary.Chapter3
{
    public partial class ParkingSpotTracker
    {
        // only including updated parts to this class
    }
}
```

In the SharedLibrary.MonoAndroid project, add a new file to the *Chapter3* folder named *ParkingSpotTracker.Extensions.cs*, which will contain the Android-specific extensions. Note that this is the same folder in which the shared *ParkingSpotTracker.cs* file is linked into. Projects can contain a mixture of linked and non-linked files, and this is a scenario where that comes in handy. Inside this file, create a new partial implementation of the ParkingSpotTracker class that adds a new method named HonkHorn (see Example 3-7).

Since this extension is specific to the Android platform, you are able to use Android's APIs for the implementation without having any impact on the other platforms. You can also solve this problem using the abstraction pattern and derived classes, but in some cases, as seen in this example, partial classes can provide a simpler alternative to combine shared code with platform-specific implementations.

Example 3-7. ParkingSpotTracker.Extensions.cs

```
namespace SharedLibrary.Chapter3
{
    public partial class ParkingSpotTracker
    {
        public void HonkHorn()
        {
            // honk the car horn
        }
    }
}
```

Conditional Compilation

One technique you may have seen if you've done other cross-platform development is *conditional compilation*. With this method, you can tell the compiler to either include or exclude blocks of code based on compilation symbols that describe the target environment. For example, most .NET projects will define a symbol named DEBUG when the project is built in the debug configuration but not in the release configuration. If you have logging code that you only want included in debug builds, you can wrap it in a conditional expression using that symbol (see Example 3-8). When the code is parsed for compilation, any code blocks surrounded by unsatisfied conditions are stripped out, and the file is compiled as if they were never there in the first place.

Example 3-8. Using the DEBUG compiler symbol

```
#ifdef DEBUG
    Console.WriteLine("This is only logged in debug mode");
#endif
```

Keep in mind that overuse of this pattern can quickly lead to code that is very difficult to read and maintain. If you find yourself using a lot of conditional compilation, it's very likely that the abstraction pattern might be a better route to go down. That said, it can be a very handy tool when you need to make minor adjustments in a shared file based on the target environment.

In your projects, you always have the option of defining any custom symbols you want, but in many cases, there are already standard predefined symbols you can use instead (see Table 3-1). Currently, MonoTouch does not provide any compiler symbols out of the box. For all applications and class libraries, Mono for Android defines the __ANDROID__ symbol. Additionally, it also defines symbols for each API level supported by your application. For example, if your application targets Froyo, which is API level 8, the build would define __ANDROID_1__ through __ANDROID_8__ since you have access to the APIs from each of those levels. In Windows Phone projects, the SILVERLIGHT and WINDOWS_PHONE symbols are provided by default for both applications and class libraries.

Table 3-1. Predefined platform compiler symbols

	iOS	Android	Windows Phone
Applications	None	__ANDROID__	SILVERLIGHT
		__ANDROID_1__	WINDOWS_PHONE
		__ANDROID_2__	
		...	
Class Libraries	None	__ANDROID__	SILVERLIGHT
		__ANDROID_1__	WINDOWS_PHONE
		__ANDROID_2__	

iOS	Android		Windows Phone
	...		

Defining custom symbols in your own projects is a simple process both in Visual Studio and MonoDevelop. In Visual Studio, open up the project's properties and go to the Build section. In there is a text box where you can define any custom symbols you want (see Figure 3-5). These symbols are defined at the build configuration level, so you can use the list at the top to switch between them. In MonoDevelop, you'll find the same settings in the Compiler section of the project properties dialog (see Figure 3-5).

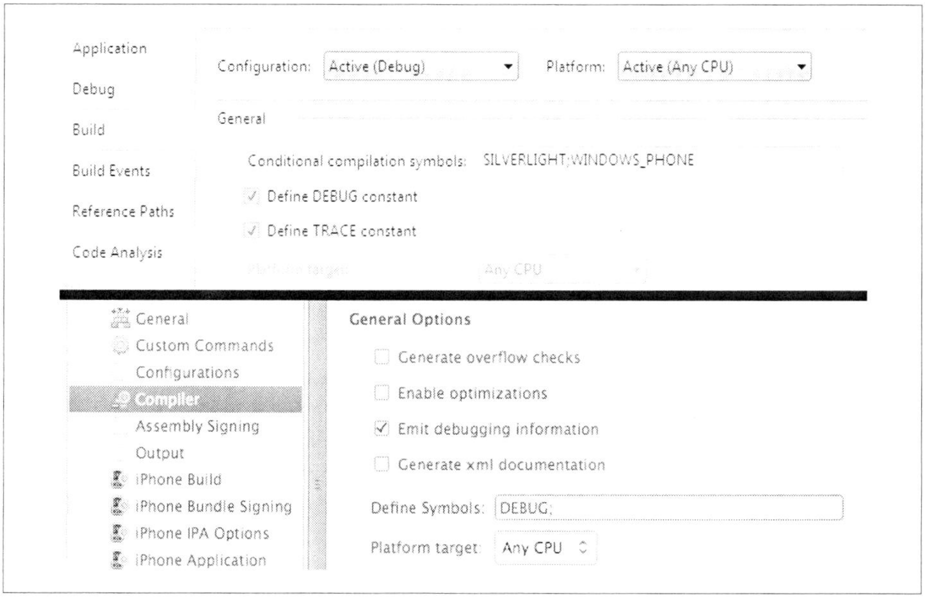

Figure 3-5. Defining symbols in Visual Studio (top) and MonoDevelop (bottom)

In the parking spot tracker, let's say you wanted to vary the interval at which you check for location updates based on the platform, and didn't want the platform to have to supply the interval itself. First, since MonoTouch does not define any symbols of its own, open the properties dialog for the SharedProject.MonoTouch project and add a new compiler symbol named MONOTOUCH. Now that there are symbols defined for all three platforms, open *ParkingSpotTracker.cs* and add a new property named UpdateIntervalSeconds. This property should return the following values based on the platform (see Example 3-9):

- Android: 30
- iOS: 45
- Windows Phone: 60

- Everything else: 120

Example 3-9. ParkingSpotTracker.cs (updates only)

```
using System;

namespace SharedLibrary.Chapter3
{
    public class ParkingSpotTracker
    {
        // only including updated parts to this class

        public int UpdateIntervalSeconds
        {
            get
            {
#if __ANDROID__
                return 30;
#elif MONOTOUCH
                return 45;
#elif WINDOWS_PHONE
                return 60;
#else
                return 120;
#endif
            }
        }
    }
}
```

Now, even though the exact same file is being shared across all three platforms, this property will look different to the compiler for each of them. When the compiler runs on the Windows Phone project, it will see the property as if it looked like Example 3-10. The #else condition here would be applied to any other platform that might use this code, such as ASP.NET or WPF.

Example 3-10. Windows Phone compiler view of UpdateIntervalSeconds

```
public int UpdateIntervalSeconds
{
    get
    {
        return 60;
    }
}
```

Summary

In this chapter, we looked at several techniques for sharing code across platforms. First, we explored the file linking features of Visual Studio and MonoDevelop in order to share entire source files across several projects without having to maintain several copies of them manually. After that, we introduced the abstraction and observer patterns, exploring how they can aid in decoupling an application's business logic from a particular platform's implementation. Following that, we looked at how to use partial classes and conditional compilation in order to share sections of a class across platforms, while also allowing for platform-specific modifications. In the remaining chapters, we will apply these techniques while building different applications that dig deeper into some common tasks you might want to perform in your apps, such as accessing the network and persisting data.

CHAPTER 4

Accessing the Network

Now that you have built applications for all three platforms and have some code sharing techniques in your tool belt, it's time to start applying them. Every good application needs to be able to connect to external resources, whether they are a complex set of web services or just a simple leaderboard. The .NET Framework provides a rich networking stack that makes it easy to interact with network resources. Since all three platforms are able to leverage the power of this framework, these built-in networking libraries provide a great common base to build upon, allowing for a large amount of code reuse between them.

Reaching into the Cloud

In this chapter, you will build a very simple Twitter client that can read in a list of tweets from a particular account and display them to the user. The user interface implementations will have to remain native to each platform, but it's possible to share all of the code needed to actually interact with Twitter's API, which will live entirely in the shared library. Even though the scope of this application is limited, it's easy to see that in a full application with an expanded set of features, the ability to reuse your code will go a long way to save time both up front and down the line.

Shared Layer

Open up the SharedLibrary project and create a new folder named *Chapter4*, where all new shared classes from this chapter will be added. Add a new class to this folder named Tweet. This will be a simple data object to hold information about a single tweet, including its ID, the time it was created, and its text content (see Example 4-1).

Example 4-1. Tweet.cs

```
using System;

namespace SharedLibrary.Chapter4
{
```

```
    public class Tweet
    {
        public long Id { get; set; }
        public DateTime CreatedAt { get; set; }
        public string Text { get; set; }
    }
}
```

Now that the data class is created, it's time to design the code to actually consume the data from Twitter's API. Twitter exposes its data through a simple REST interface, which allows you to request data by using different URLs that it defined, just as you would with a web site. To get a list of tweets from the O'Reilly Media account, you can use the following URL:

https://api.twitter.com/1/statuses/user_timeline.xml?screen_name=OReillyMedia

Example 4-2 shows what the resulting XML will look like. The actual response from Twitter will include a lot more information that can be ignored for the purposes of this application. The XML in Example 4-2 only includes the fields relevant to this chapter.

Example 4-2. Sample XML response from Twitter (simplified)

```
<?xml version="1.0" encoding="UTF-8"?>
<statuses type="array">
  <status>
    <created_at>Mon Dec 12 11:28:54 +0000 2011</created_at>
    <id>111111111111111111</id>
    <text>...</text>
  </status>
  <status>
    <created_at>Sun Dec 11 16:20:10 +0000 2011</created_at>
    <id>222222222222222222</id>
    <text>...</text>
  </status>
</statuses>
```

Add a new class named `TwitterClient` to the *Chapter4* folder which will handle all communication with the Twitter API (see Example 4-3). The client needs to provide one method named, `GetTweetsForUser`, which takes in a Twitter username and returns a list of tweets for that user.

Example 4-3. TwitterClient.cs

```
using System;
using System.Collections.Generic;
using System.Linq;
using System.Net;
using System.Threading;
using System.Xml.Linq;

namespace SharedLibrary.Chapter4
{
    public class TwitterClient
```

```
    {
        private const string _baseUrl = "https://api.twitter.com/1/statuses/";

        public void GetTweetsForUser(string user, Action<IList<Tweet>> callback) ❶
        {
            string url = _baseUrl + "user_timeline.xml?screen_name=" +
Uri.EscapeUriString(user);
            var client = new WebClient(); ❷

            client.DownloadStringCompleted +=
                (sender, args) =>
                {
                    var tweets =
                        XDocument
                            .Parse(args.Result) ❸
                            .Root
                            .Elements("status")
                            .Select(status => new Tweet ❹
                            {
                                Id = long.Parse(status.Element("id").Value),
                                CreatedAt =
DateTime.ParseExact(status.Element("created_at").Value,
                                            "ddd MMM dd HH:mm:ss zz00 yyyy", null),
                                Text = status.Element("text").Value
                            })
                            .ToList();

                    callback(tweets); ❺
                };

            client.DownloadStringAsync(new Uri(url)); ❻
        }
    }
}
```

❶ Define the GetTweetsForUser method, which takes in the username and also a call-back method for processing the results.

❷ Since the System.Net namespace is available to all three platforms, you can leverage the standard WebClient class to handle communicating with the API.

❸ Use the built-in .NET XML libraries for parsing the XML response.

❹ LINQ-to-XML is available for all platforms as well, so use that to transform each XML status element into a Tweet object.

❺ Once the list of tweets has been processed, send that through to the provided call-back method.

❻ Finally, tell the WebClient object to begin the request asynchronously.

Looking at this code, one thing you might be wondering is the reason for making the request asynchronously and passing the result back through the use of a callback, rather than using the return value of the method. Either style would work perfectly fine, but each comes with its own set of advantages and difficulties. Synchronous code is generally much easier to read and test but will be executed on the same thread it is called from, which in most cases will be the UI thread. If the UI thread of an application is locked up for some period of time, the entire application will appear unresponsive to the user during that time. This means that each calling platform would need to remember to move this method call into a background thread to avoid locking up the application for the duration of the request. By implementing the method asynchronously, as is done in this example, the request will automatically happen in a background thread. This helps to simplify the application code on each platform since it won't need to worry about spawning and managing new threads.

That's all the code needed to interact with Twitter's API for the purposes of this application. As you can see, the code is focused entirely on retrieving a list of tweets across the network without caring how they are being used or displayed. Make sure to add links to these files in the SharedLibrary.MonoTouch, SharedLibrary.MonoAndroid, and SharedLibrary.WindowsPhone projects so that all platforms can access them. You can refer back to Chapter 3 if you need to review how to link files between projects. You'll also need to add references to System.Xml and System.Xml.Linq to each project in order for them to compile correctly.

iOS

Now that the shared layer is built, it's time to write some apps on top of it, starting with iOS. Create a new empty iPhone project named Chapter4.MonoTouchApp. Add the SharedLibrary.MonoTouch project to the solution and add a reference to it from Chapter4.MonoTouchApp so that the application can access the Twitter client.

The user interface for this application will be a list of tweets. In iOS applications, lists are typically implemented using a UITableView, which is essentially a table with just one column. It is roughly analogous to list controls you may be familiar with on other platforms. Each row in the table is represented by UITableViewCell objects, which can be customized according to what the application needs to display. One way to add a UITableView to an interface is to use Interface Builder, as in Chapter 2. However, for cases like this where the entire interface is a list, iOS includes a specialized view controller type, UITableViewController, to help simplify the process.

Add a new class to the project named TwitterViewController, which should extend UITableViewController. Once the view loads, the application should show a loading indicator to the user while it downloads the list of tweets, and then show the list once the results come back (see Example 4-4).

Example 4-4. TwitterViewController.cs

```
using MonoTouch.UIKit;
using SharedLibrary.Chapter4;

namespace Chapter4.MonoTouchApp
```

```
{
    public class TwitterViewController : UITableViewController ❶
    {
        private TwitterClient _client;

        public override void ViewDidLoad()
        {
            base.ViewDidLoad();

            _client = new TwitterClient(); ❷

            var loading = new UIAlertView("Downloading Tweets", ❸
                                         "Please wait...",
                                         null, null, null);
            loading.Show();

            var indicator = new
UIActivityIndicatorView(UIActivityIndicatorViewStyle.WhiteLarge);
            indicator.Center = new System.Drawing.PointF(loading.Bounds.Width / 2,
                                                loading.Bounds.Size.Height - 40);
            indicator.StartAnimating();
            loading.AddSubview(indicator); ❹

            _client.GetTweetsForUser("OReillyMedia", tweets => ❺
            {
                InvokeOnMainThread(() => ❻
                {
                    TableView.Source = new TwitterTableViewSource(tweets);
                    TableView.ReloadData();
                    loading.DismissWithClickedButtonIndex(0, true);
                });
            });
        }
    }
}
```

❶ Extend the `UITableViewController` class.

❷ Create a new instance of `TwitterClient`.

❸ Show a dialog box that displays a message to the user while downloading the tweets.

❹ Add an animated loading indicator to the dialog.

❺ Start downloading tweets for the OReillyMedia account and assign a callback for the results.

❻ On the UI thread, display the results in the table and hide the loading indicator.

The most interesting code here is inside the callback for processing the list of tweets. As discussed earlier, you want to keep all long-running operations happening in background threads in order to keep the application as responsive as possible for the user. However, once the result comes back and you want to make updates to the interface, those updates should happen back on the UI thread. In iOS, you can explicitly say that a block of code should run on the UI thread by wrapping it in a call to InvokeOnMainThread().

The other part of this callback that won't look familiar is the use of the TwitterTable ViewSource class, which hasn't been defined yet. Add a new class to the project named TwitterTableViewSource that extends the UITableViewSource class. iOS provides two classes for specifying how a UITableView should render: UITableViewDelegate and UITableViewDataSource. Both classes are available in MonoTouch, but since they are very similar, MonoTouch also provides the UITableViewSource class that combines them to simplify the process. By overriding different methods in this class, you can provide the height of a row, the contents of a cell, what to do when the user selects one of the rows, and a number of other options (see Example 4-5).

Example 4-5. TwitterTableViewSource.cs

```
using System.Collections.Generic;
using MonoTouch.Foundation;
using MonoTouch.UIKit;
using SharedLibrary.Chapter4;

namespace Chapter4.MonoTouchApp
{
    public class TwitterTableViewSource : UITableViewSource
    {
        private readonly IList<Tweet> _tweets;
        private const string TweetCell = "TweetCell";

        public TwitterTableViewSource(IList<Tweet> tweets) ❶
        {
            _tweets = tweets;
        }

        public override int RowsInSection(UITableView tableView, int section) ❷
        {
            return _tweets.Count;
        }

        public override float GetHeightForRow(UITableView tableView, NSIndexPath indexPath)
❸
        {
            return 60;
        }

        public override UITableViewCell GetCell(UITableView tableView, NSIndexPath
indexPath) ❹
        {
            var cell = tableView.DequeueReusableCell(TweetCell) ❺
                    ?? new UITableViewCell(UITableViewCellStyle.Subtitle, TweetCell);
            var tweet = _tweets[indexPath.Row];

            cell.TextLabel.Text = tweet.Text; ❻
            cell.DetailTextLabel.Text = tweet.CreatedAt.ToLocalTime().ToString(); ❼
```

```
            return cell;
        }

        public override void RowSelected(UITableView tableView, NSIndexPath indexPath) ❽
        {
            var selectedTweet = _tweets[indexPath.Row];
            new UIAlertView("Full Tweet", selectedTweet.Text,
                        null, "Ok", null).Show();
        }
    }
}
```

❶ Require that a list of tweets be supplied via the constructor.

❷ The RowsInTable() method declares how many rows a table section has. Since this table has only one section, it is equal to the number of tweets received.

❸ For this application all rows should have the same height, so GetHeightForRow() returns a constant value.

❹ The GetCell() method is called once per row in the table, and tells the table how to render that row.

❺ Create a table cell using the built-in Subtitle style, reusing an existing cell if possible to be more efficient.

❻ Set the primary text of the cell to be the text of the tweet.

❼ Set the secondary text of the cell to be the date and time the tweet was created, converted to the user's local time.

❽ When the user selects a row in the table, the RowSelected() method specifies how to process it. This application shows an alert to the user containing the full text of the tweet.

One important thing to note here is the use of DequeueReusableCell() inside of the GetCell() method. It's possible for a list to contain a very large number of elements depending on what you're showing the user, but only a small fraction of them will be visible at any given time due to the size of the screen. Using DequeueReusableCell() allows the OS to reuse cells it has already allocated if they are no longer visible to the user in order to avoid having to allocate memory for every cell in the table. Even if your table contains multiple cell layouts you can simply assign different keys to each of them and still allow for cell reusability when possible. When there is no cell available to be reused DequeueReusableCell() will return null and a new cell should be constructed.

All that's left to do is tell the application to load a new TwitterViewController when it starts. Open up *AppDelegate.cs* and modify the FinishedLaunching() method to show the view (see Example 4-6). Now you can start the application, which should look similar to Figure 4-1.

Example 4-6. AppDelegate.cs

```
using MonoTouch.Foundation;
using MonoTouch.UIKit;

namespace Chapter4.MonoTouchApp
{
    [Register ("AppDelegate")]
    public partial class AppDelegate : UIApplicationDelegate
    {
        private UIWindow _window;
        private TwitterViewController _twitterViewController;

        public override bool FinishedLaunching(UIApplication app, NSDictionary options)
        {
            _window = new UIWindow (UIScreen.MainScreen.Bounds);

            _twitterViewController = new TwitterViewController();
            _window.RootViewController = _twitterViewController;

            _window.MakeKeyAndVisible ();

            return true;
        }
    }
}
```

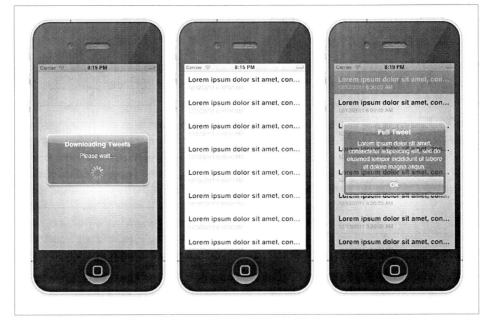

Figure 4-1. Twitter app for iOS

Android

Now let's move on to the Android app. Create a new Mono for Android application project named `Chapter4.MonoAndroid`. Just as with the iOS application, add the `SharedLibrary.MonoAndroid` project to the solution and reference it from `Chapter4.MonoAndroid`. You can remove any activities and layout resources added by the project template to start from a fresh slate.

Since the application needs to access the Internet, Android requires that you explicitly request that permission in the application's *AndroidManifest.xml* file. Any permissions you request will be shown to the user when they install the app, so be careful to only include what you need. Since Mono for Android tries to generate as much of this file for you as possible, you can request permissions through the project's properties dialog.

Open up the project properties and select Android Manifest if using Visual Studio, or Mono for Android Application if you're using MonoDevelop. If there isn't already a manifest for the project, which is likely the case since this is a fresh project, it will give you the option to create one. Go ahead and create the file, since this application will need to make changes to it. Once the file is created, you should see different options, including a list of permissions required for the application. From this list, check off the box for the `INTERNET` permission (see Figure 4-2).

Figure 4-2. Requesting permission to access the internet

In the *Resources/Layout* folder, add a new Android layout file named *Twitter.axml*. Add a `ListView` element to the layout, which will serve as the list of tweets to be shown to the user (see Example 4-7). In the same folder, add a second layout file named *Tweet.axml* that will be used for each tweet in the list. In this layout, add two

TextView elements, one for the tweet's text and the other for the time it was created (see Example 4-8). For both of these layouts, each element should be assigned an ID so that it is accessible from the application code.

Example 4-7. Twitter.axml

```xml
<?xml version="1.0" encoding="utf-8"?>
<LinearLayout xmlns:android="http://schemas.android.com/apk/res/android"
    android:orientation="vertical"
    android:layout_width="fill_parent"
    android:layout_height="fill_parent">
    <ListView
        android:id="@+id/Tweets"
        android:layout_width="match_parent"
        android:layout_height="wrap_content" />
</LinearLayout>
```

Example 4-8. Tweet.axml

```xml
<?xml version="1.0" encoding="utf-8"?>
<LinearLayout xmlns:android="http://schemas.android.com/apk/res/android"
    android:orientation="vertical"
    android:layout_width="fill_parent"
    android:layout_height="fill_parent">
    <TextView
        android:id="@+id/Text"
        android:layout_width="match_parent"
        android:layout_height="wrap_content"
        android:ellipsize="end"
        android:singleLine="true"
        android:textAppearance="?android:attr/textAppearanceMedium"
        android:padding="5dip" />
    <TextView
        android:id="@+id/CreatedAt"
        android:layout_width="match_parent"
        android:layout_height="wrap_content"
        android:padding="5dip" />
</LinearLayout>
```

Next, add a new activity to the application named `TwitterActivity`. As before, once the activity is created, it should display a progress dialog to the user while downloading the list of tweets. This activity display the list to the user when the data is ready (see Example 4-9).

Example 4-9. TwitterActivity.cs

```csharp
using Android.App;
using Android.OS;
using Android.Widget;
using SharedLibrary.Chapter4;

namespace Chapter4.MonoAndroidApp
{
    [Activity (Label = "\\@OReillyMedia", MainLauncher = true)] ❶
```

```
public class TwitterActivity : Activity
{
    protected override void OnCreate(Bundle bundle)
    {
        base.OnCreate (bundle);

        SetContentView (Resource.Layout.Twitter); ❷

        var client = new TwitterClient(); ❸

        var loading = ProgressDialog.Show(this, ❹
                                    "Downloading Tweets",
                                    "Please wait...", true);

        client.GetTweetsForUser("OReillyMedia", tweets => ❺
        {
            RunOnUiThread (() => ❻
            {
                var tweetList = FindViewById<ListView>(Resource.Id.Tweets); ❼
                tweetList.Adapter = new TweetListAdapter(this, tweets); ❽
                tweetList.ItemClick += (object sender, ItemEventArgs e) => ❾
                {
                    var selectedTweet = tweets[e.Position];

                    new AlertDialog.Builder(this)
                        .SetTitle("Full Tweet")
                        .SetMessage(selectedTweet.Text)
                        .SetPositiveButton("Ok", delegate { })
                        .Show();
                };

                loading.Hide();
            });
        });
    }
}
}
```

❶ Decorate the activity with `ActivityAttribute` to generate the proper entry in *AndroidManifest.xml*.

❷ Set the activity's layout to *Twitter.axml*.

❸ Create a new instance of `TwitterClient`.

❹ Show a progress dialog to the user while downloading the list of tweets.

❺ Start downloading tweets for the OReillyMedia account and assign a callback for the results.

❻ Make sure to update the UI from the UI thread.

❼ Get a reference to the list in the layout.

❽ Set the list's adapter so that it displays the data.

❾ When any list item is clicked on, display an alert dialog containing the full text of the tweet.

Just like in iOS, Android provides its own method to allow a background thread to update the UI: RunOnUiThread(). This is important because if your application does not respond to user input for five seconds, it will show an alert to the user saying it has stopped responding, and offers them the option of forcing the app to close. Even though the limit here is five seconds, in reality you never want to come anywhere close to that threshold. You should always strive to keep your application as responsive as possible.

In the callback method, you may have noticed the use of a class named TweetListAdapter, which has not been defined yet. Go ahead and add a new class named TweetListAdapter to the project. As the name implies, this is a class that will be used to take the list of tweets returned and expose them in a way the ListView understands. In Android, each item in a list can be any view object, so it can be anything from a single TextView to a layout containing any number of objects. Items in the list of tweets will be inflated using the layout defined in *Tweet.axml* (see Example 4-11).

Example 4-10. TweetListAdapter.cs

```
using System.Collections.Generic;
using Android.App;
using Android.Views;
using Android.Widget;
using SharedLibrary.Chapter4;

namespace Chapter4.MonoAndroidApp
{
    public class TweetListAdapter : BaseAdapter<Tweet> ❶
    {
        private readonly Activity _context;
        private readonly IList<Tweet> _tweets;

        public TweetListAdapter(Activity context, IList<Tweet> tweets) ❷
        {
            _context = context;
            _tweets = tweets;
        }

        public override View GetView(int position, View convertView, ViewGroup parent) ❸
        {
            var view = convertView ❹
                        ?? _context.LayoutInflater.Inflate(Resource.Layout.Tweet, null);
            var tweet = _tweets[position];

            view.FindViewById<TextView>(Resource.Id.Text).Text = tweet.Text; ❺
            view.FindViewById<TextView>(Resource.Id.CreatedAt).Text = ❻
                tweet.CreatedAt.ToLocalTime().ToString();

            return view;
        }
```

```
    public override int Count ❼
    {
        get { return _tweets.Count; }
    }

    public override long GetItemId(int position) ❽
    {
        return position;
    }

    public override Tweet this[int position] ❾
    {
        get { return _tweets[position]; }
    }
  }
}
```

❶ Extend the BaseAdapter class, strongly typing it with the type Tweet.

❷ In the constructor, require an activity context and a list of tweets.

❸ The GetView() is what provides the list with a view to display, and is called every time a list item is being created.

❹ If there is a value for convertView, use that instead of inflating a brand new View.

❺ Update the first TextView to contain the tweet's text.

❻ Update the second TextView to contain the date and time the tweet was created, converted to the user's local time.

❼ Specify how many items are in this list.

❽ GetItemId() specifies an ID for a given row. For this application, simply return the position in the list.

❾ Override the array index operator for this class so that it returns the item at a specified position in the list.

Inside the implementation of GetView(), make note of the use of the convertView parameter. As in the iOS application, you don't want to have to allocate list items for every element in a very long list when only a few will be displayed at any given time. If a view has already been inflated that can be reused, it will be passed in as convert View. If the parameter is null, use the provided activity to inflate a new View object from the layout. In Java, this class would normally be implemented as an anonymous implementation, which automatically has access to the outer activity. Since C# doesn't support this feature, you have to pass in the activity to the adapter as seen here.

That's everything required for the Android application. Start it up in the emulator and it should look similar to Figure 4-3.

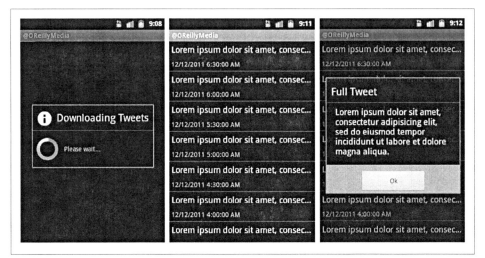

Figure 4-3. Twitter app for Android

Windows Phone

Finally, let's create the same application for Windows Phone. Create a new Windows Phone application project named `Chapter4.WindowsPhoneApp`. Add the `SharedLibrary.WindowsPhone` project to the solution and reference it from `Chapter4.WindowsPhoneApp`.

Open up *MainPage.xaml*, and modify it to look like Example 4-11:

Example 4-11. MainPage.xaml

```xml
<phone:PhoneApplicationPage
    x:Class="Chapter4.WindowsPhoneApp.MainPage"
    xmlns="http://schemas.microsoft.com/winfx/2006/xaml/presentation"
    xmlns:x="http://schemas.microsoft.com/winfx/2006/xaml"
    xmlns:phone="clr-namespace:Microsoft.Phone.Controls;assembly=Microsoft.Phone"
    xmlns:shell="clr-namespace:Microsoft.Phone.Shell;assembly=Microsoft.Phone"
    xmlns:d="http://schemas.microsoft.com/expression/blend/2008"
    xmlns:mc="http://schemas.openxmlformats.org/markup-compatibility/2006"
    mc:Ignorable="d" d:DesignWidth="480" d:DesignHeight="768"
    FontFamily="{StaticResource PhoneFontFamilyNormal}"
    FontSize="{StaticResource PhoneFontSizeNormal}"
    Foreground="{StaticResource PhoneForegroundBrush}"
    SupportedOrientations="Portrait" Orientation="Portrait"
    shell:SystemTray.IsVisible="True">

    <Grid x:Name="LayoutRoot" Background="Transparent">
        <Grid.RowDefinitions>
            <RowDefinition Height="Auto"/>
            <RowDefinition Height="*"/>
        </Grid.RowDefinitions>
```

```xaml
        <StackPanel x:Name="TitlePanel" Grid.Row="0" Margin="12,17,0,28">
            <TextBlock x:Name="ApplicationTitle" Text="Twitter" Style="{StaticResource
PhoneTextNormalStyle}"/> ❶
            <TextBlock x:Name="PageTitle" Text="@OReillyMedia" Margin="9,-7,0,0"
Style="{StaticResource PhoneTextTitle1Style}"/> ❷
        </StackPanel>

        <Grid x:Name="ContentPanel" Grid.Row="1" Margin="12,0,12,0">
            <StackPanel x:Name="Loading"> ❸
                <ProgressBar IsIndeterminate="True" />
                <TextBlock TextAlignment="Center" Text="Downloading tweets, please wait..." />
            </StackPanel>
            <ListBox x:Name="Items" Margin="0,0,-12,0" ItemsSource="{Binding}"
SelectionChanged="TweetSelected"> ❹
                <ListBox.ItemTemplate>
                    <DataTemplate>
                        <StackPanel Margin="0,15,0,15">
                            <TextBlock Text="{Binding Text}" TextTrimming="WordEllipsis"
Style="{StaticResource PhoneTextNormalStyle}"/> ❺
                            <TextBlock Text="{Binding CreatedAt}" Style="{StaticResource
PhoneTextSmallStyle}"/> ❻
                        </StackPanel>
                    </DataTemplate>
                </ListBox.ItemTemplate>
            </ListBox>
        </Grid>
    </Grid>
</phone:PhoneApplicationPage>
```

❶ In the title panel, set the application's title to "Twitter."

❷ Also in the title panel, change the page's title to "@OReillyMedia."

❸ Add a StackPanel that contains a progress bar and text informing the user that the download is happening.

❹ Add a ListBox to display the list of tweets returned from Twitter, attaching an event handler to when a tweet is selected.

❺ For each tweet, display the tweet's text first.

❻ Below that, in a smaller font display the time and date which it was created, converted to the user's local time.

Next, open up the page's code-behind file, *MainPage.xaml.cs*. When the page is loaded, it should display the progress indicator to the user while downloading the list of tweets, and then show the list when the data is ready (see Example 4-12).

Example 4-12. MainPage.xaml.cs

```csharp
using System.Windows;
using System.Windows.Controls;
using Microsoft.Phone.Controls;
using SharedLibrary.Chapter4;
```

```
namespace Chapter4.WindowsPhoneApp
{
    public partial class MainPage : PhoneApplicationPage
    {
        public MainPage()
        {
            InitializeComponent();
        }

        protected override void OnNavigatedTo(System.Windows.Navigation.NavigationEventArgs
e)
        {
            base.OnNavigatedTo(e);

            var client = new TwitterClient(); ❶

            client.GetTweetsForUser("OReillyMedia", tweets => ❷
            {
                Deployment.Current.Dispatcher.BeginInvoke(() => ❸
                {
                    DataContext = tweets; ❹
                    Loading.Visibility = Visibility.Collapsed; ❺
                });
            });
        }

        private void TweetSelected(object sender, SelectionChangedEventArgs e)
        {
            var tweet = (Tweet)e.AddedItems[0];

            MessageBox.Show(tweet.Text, "Full Tweet", MessageBoxButton.OK); ❻
        }
    }
}
```

❶ Create a new instance of `TwitterClient`.

❷ Start downloading tweets for the OReillyMedia account and assign a callback for the results.

❸ Make sure to update the UI from the UI thread.

❹ Set the page's `DataContext` to the list of tweets to trigger data binding.

❺ Hide the progress indicator.

❻ When a tweet is selected, display a message box containing its full text.

Windows Phone, just like iOS and Android, provides a mechanism to invoke a block of code on the UI thread when running on a background thread by using `Deployment.Current.Dispatcher.BeginInvoke()`. This allows the application to remain responsive and display the progress indicator instead of freezing for the duration of the request. Thanks to XAML's powerful data binding capabilities, that's all that needs to be done to display the results in the user interface. If you run the application in the emulator, it should look like Figure 4-4.

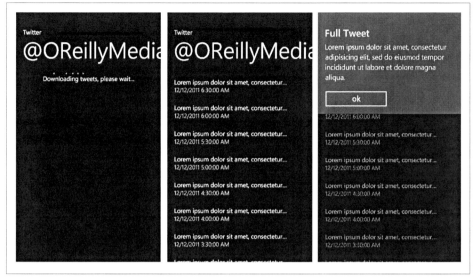

Figure 4-4. Twitter app for Windows Phone

Notifying the User Interface

Suppose that you wanted to extend the application to show the user an alert whenever somebody mentions her on Twitter. The logic to check with Twitter for mentions would ideally remain in the shared layer so that it can be reused across all platforms. This means that the check needs to be platform-independent, but each platform still needs to be able to know when it occurs so that it can notify the user. This is a great example of a time when the observer pattern discussed in Chapter 3 can come in handy. `TwitterClient` can expose an event that it publishes when a mention is detected, and each application can subscribe to the event and alert the user.

Shared Layer

First, add a new class to the *Chapter4* folder named `MentionEventArgs`, which will represent the data sent back to the application when the event is fired. It should include a `Tweet` object (the same type created in the first section) containing information about the mention (see Example 4-13).

Example 4-13. MentionEventArgs.cs

```
using System;

namespace SharedLibrary.Chapter4
```

```
{
    public class MentionEventArgs : EventArgs
    {
        public Tweet Tweet { get; private set; }

        public MentionEventArgs(Tweet tweet)
        {
            Tweet = tweet;
        }
    }
}
```

Now open up *TwitterClient.cs* and modify it to look like Example 4-14. The example only includes new code being added to the class, so append this to what is already in that class.

Example 4-14. TwitterClient.cs (updates only)

```
using System;
using System.Collections.Generic;
using System.Linq;
using System.Net;
using System.Threading;
using System.Xml.Linq;

namespace SharedLibrary.Chapter4
{
    public class TwitterClient
    {
        public event EventHandler<MentionEventArgs> MentionReceived; ❶

        public TwitterClient()
        {
            new Timer(delegate ❷
            {
                var mention = new Tweet ❸
                {
                    Id = 42,
                    CreatedAt = DateTime.Now,
                    Text = "This is a fake mention"
                };

                if (MentionReceived != null) ❹
                {
                    MentionReceived(this, new MentionEventArgs(mention));
                }
            }, null, 15 * 1000, Timeout.Infinite); ❺
        }

        // ...code from last section...
    }
}
```

❶ Define the MentionReceived event, supplying MentionEventArgs as its argument type.

❷ In the constructor, start a timer to pretend a mention is received.

❸ Create a fake mention, assigning values for its properties.

❹ If there are any subscribers to the event, publish the event to them.

❺ Set the timer to fire once after 15 seconds.

To keep things simple, this example uses a Timer to fake the event of receiving a mention instead of getting bogged down in Twitter specifics. Fifteen seconds after the instance of TwitterClient is created, the timer will elapse and any subscribers to the event will be notified that a mention was received. Each application is then free to notify the user in any way it wants, allowing for fully native behavior. Add links to both of these files in all three platform-shared library projects.

iOS

Open up *TwitterViewController.cs* and attach a handler to the client's MentionReceived event in the ViewDidLoad() method. When the event is received, show a new UIAlertView containing the tweet's text (see Example 4-15). Remember that the callback will happen on a background thread, so be sure to show the alert back on the UI thread. When you run the application and the timer elapses, it should look like Figure 4-5.

Example 4-15. TwitterViewController.cs (updates only)

```
using MonoTouch.UIKit;
using SharedLibrary.Chapter4;

namespace Chapter4.MonoTouchApp
{
    public class TwitterViewController : UITableViewController
    {
        public override void ViewDidLoad()
        {
            // ...code from last section...

            _client.MentionReceived += (object sender, MentionEventArgs args) =>
            {
                InvokeOnMainThread(() =>
                    new UIAlertView("Mention Received", args.Tweet.Text,
                                null, "Ok", null).Show());
            };
        }
    }
}
```

Figure 4-5. Mention received on iOS

Android

Back in the Android application, modify `TwitterActivity` and attach a handler to the client's `MentionReceived` event in `OnCreate()`. When the event is fired, show an alert dialog with the tweet's text (see Example 4-16), making sure to do it on the UI thread. Running the application should result in something similar to Figure 4-6.

Example 4-16. TwitterActivity.cs (updates only)

```
using Android.App;
using Android.OS;
using Android.Widget;
```

```
using SharedLibrary.Chapter4;

namespace Chapter4.MonoAndroidApp
{
    [Activity (Label = "\\@OReillyMedia", MainLauncher = true)]
    public class TwitterActivity : Activity
    {
        protected override void OnCreate(Bundle bundle)
        {
            // ...code from last section...

            client.MentionReceived += (object sender, MentionEventArgs args) =>
            {
                RunOnUiThread(() =>
                {
                    new AlertDialog.Builder(this)
                        .SetTitle ("Mention Received")
                        .SetMessage(args.Tweet.Text)
                        .SetPositiveButton("Ok", delegate { })
                        .Show();
                });
            };
        }
    }
}
```

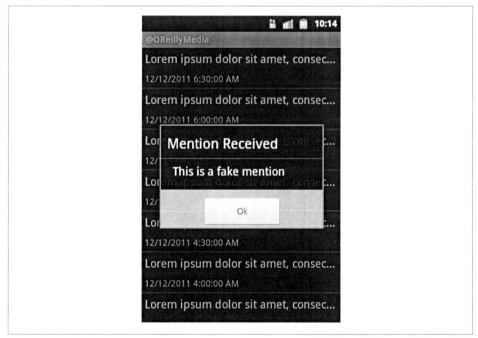

Figure 4-6. Mention received on Android

Windows Phone

Lastly, in the Windows Phone application, open *MainPage.xaml.cs*. In the OnNaviga tedTo() method, show a message box when a mention is received, again being careful to execute the code on the UI thread. Running the application in the emulator should look like Figure 4-7.

Example 4-17. MainPage.xaml.cs (updates only)

```
using System.Windows;
using System.Windows.Controls;
using Microsoft.Phone.Controls;
using SharedLibrary.Chapter4;

namespace Chapter4.WindowsPhoneApp
{
    public partial class MainPage : PhoneApplicationPage
    {
        protected override void OnNavigatedTo(System.Windows.Navigation.NavigationEventArgs
e)
        {
            // ...code from last section...

            client.MentionReceived += delegate(object sender, MentionEventArgs args)
            {
                Deployment.Current.Dispatcher.BeginInvoke(() =>
                {
                    MessageBox.Show(args.Tweet.Text, "Mention Received",
                                    MessageBoxButton.OK);
                });
            };
        }
    }
}
```

Summary

In this chapter, you created a simple application that communicates with the Twitter API over the Internet to download a list of tweets for a given user. All code involved with accessing the network and API was entirely contained to the shared library, and worked seamlessly across all platforms. Each application implemented a native user interface on top of that shared layer. While the implementations were similar across all of them, there is nothing preventing you from creating entirely different interfaces and user experiences for each of them. The observer pattern introduced in the last chapter was also leveraged to allow the shared layer to publish notifications to the application that a mention was received. In the next chapter, we will explore some options for persisting data in your applications, making use of both the filesystem and local databases.

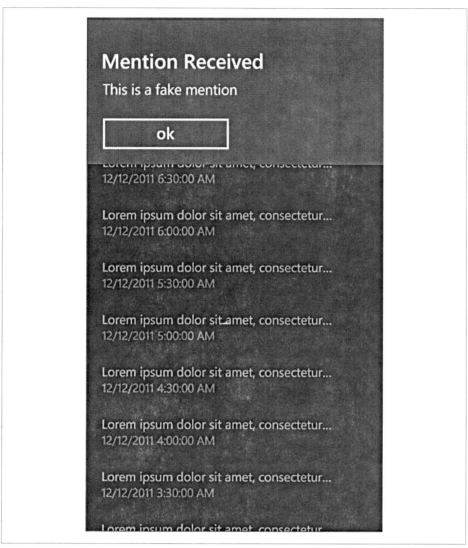

Figure 4-7. Mention received on Windows Phone

CHAPTER 5

Storing Data

Whether it is saving a user's input or caching data pulled down from a web service, every application needs some way to persist its data for retrieval. There are various options available for storing data in your applications. This chapter will explore two of the primary methods for doing so: reading and writing files to the filesystem and making use of the device's local database. Each platform provides different capabilities for both the filesystem and databases, but thanks to the shared usage of the .NET framework, there is still plenty of potential for code reuse across each of them.

In this chapter, we will be building a simple note-taking application where the user can save notes, each consisting of a title and body text. The user will also be able to view a list of his saved notes and have the option of viewing or deleting them. Before implementing the actual data persistence, we will first build the sample application, demonstrating how to leverage the abstraction pattern to allow the application to be ignorant of those implementations.

Following that, we will add an implementation to save the data to the local filesystem. In addition to that implementation, we will look at the differences in filesystem access across platforms, and what you can do on each of them. Finally, we will extend the application to use a local database to perform the same task, again discussing the important platform capabilities and differences to be aware of. While building these applications, we will start to dive a little deeper into each platform, introducing you to some elements not touched upon in previous chapters.

Project Setup

Before diving into the actual storage implementations, let's start out by creating the actual applications for each platform first. In doing so, we'll design the applications in such a way that they are not tied to any particular storage implementation. The reason for this is that they will only care about the actual data, and not how it is stored. Keep in mind that the applications won't actually be functional until we add these implementations in later sections of the chapter.

Shared Layer

Open up the `SharedLibrary` project and create a new folder named *Chapter5*. Add a new class to this folder named `Note`. This will hold the data for a single note, including its ID, title and contents (see Example 5-1).

Example 5-1. Note.cs

```
namespace SharedLibrary.Chapter5
{
    public class Note
    {
        public long Id { get; set; }
        public string Title { get; set; }
        public string Contents { get; set; }
    }
}
```

In order to allow the applications to make use of these different storage mechanisms without worrying about the implementation, create a new interface named `INoteRepository` that will outline the data access methods the applications need (see Example 5-2). This includes methods of retrieving a list of all notes, adding a new note, and deleting a particular note.

Example 5-2. INoteRepository.cs

```
using System.Collections.Generic;

namespace SharedLibrary.Chapter5
{
    public interface INoteRepository
    {
        IList<Note> GetAllNotes();
        void Add(string title, string contents);
        void Delete(long id);
    }
}
```

That's all the shared layer needs for the time being. Don't forget to add links to these files in the `SharedLibrary.MonoTouch`, `SharedLibrary.MonoAndroid`, and `SharedLibrary.WindowsPhone` projects.

iOS

Create a new empty iPhone project named `Chapter5.MonoTouchApp`, adding the `SharedLibrary.MonoTouch` project to the solution and referencing it. First, open *AppDelegate.cs* and add a static `INoteRepository` property to the class (see Example 5-3). This is what other classes in the application will use to access the repository. Since it uses the interface, the rest of the application is able to depend on that interface instead of an explicit implementation. Define a `UINavigationController` as the window's view, adding to it a new instance of NoteListViewController, a view controller that will show the list of saved notes. This class will be defined later on.

Example 5-3. AppDelegate.cs

```
using MonoTouch.Foundation;
using MonoTouch.UIKit;
using SharedLibrary.Chapter5;

namespace Chapter5.MonoTouchApp
{
    [Register ("AppDelegate")]
    public partial class AppDelegate : UIApplicationDelegate
    {
        private UIWindow _window;
        private UINavigationController _navigationController;

        public static INoteRepository NoteRepository { get; private set; }

        public override bool FinishedLaunching(UIApplication app, NSDictionary options)
        {
            _window = new UIWindow (UIScreen.MainScreen.Bounds);

            _navigationController = new UINavigationController();
            _navigationController.PushViewController(new NoteListViewController(), false);

            _window.RootViewController = _navigationController;

            _window.MakeKeyAndVisible ();

            return true;
        }
    }
}
```

There are a few screens required by the application, the first of which is a view of a particular note, showing its title and contents. Add a new iPhone View Controller to the project, naming it ViewNoteViewController. Double-click on *ViewNoteViewController.xib* to load the view in Interface Builder. Add two labels to the view, one above the other (see Figure 5-1), to hold the text for the note's title and contents. Since the text for these labels will be set from code, add outlets for the labels named NoteTitle and NoteContents, respectively. You can refer back to Chapter 2 if you need a reminder on how to set these up. After you've wired these up, open up *ViewNoteViewController.cs* and modify it to look like Example 5-4:

Example 5-4. ViewNoteViewController.cs

```
using MonoTouch.UIKit;
using SharedLibrary.Chapter5;

namespace Chapter5.MonoTouchApp
{
    public partial class ViewNoteViewController : UIViewController
```

```
{
    private readonly Note _note;

    public ViewNoteViewController(Note note) ❶
        : base ("ViewNoteViewController", null)
    {
        _note = note;
    }

    public override void ViewDidLoad()
    {
        base.ViewDidLoad ();

        Title = "Note";

        NoteTitle.Text = _note.Title; ❷
        NoteContents.Text = _note.Contents; ❸
        NoteContents.SizeToFit(); ❹

        var deleteButton = ❺
            new UIBarButtonItem(UIBarButtonSystemItem.Trash,
                                delegate
                                {
                                    AppDelegate.NoteRepository.Delete(_note.Id);

                                    NavigationController.PopViewControllerAnimated(true);
                                });

        NavigationItem.RightBarButtonItem = deleteButton;
    }
}
}
```

❶ Pass in a Note in the constructor, storing it for use in ViewDidLoad().

❷ Set the title label's text to the note's title.

❸ Set the contents label's text to the note's contents.

❹ Tell the contents label to expand to account for long blocks of text.

❺ Show a delete button in the upper right corner of the view.

A common convention in iOS applications is to show an action button in the upper right when applicable, such as the option to add or delete an item or refresh the view. In order to follow the native UI patterns, this application makes use of that as well. When the button is tapped, the note is deleted using the shared repository, and the application navigates back to the list of saved notes.

The second screen needed in the application is one where the user can enter a new note and save it. Add a new iPhone View Controller to the project named AddNoteViewController. Double-click on *AddNoteViewController.xib* to load it in Interface Builder. In the view, add in two text fields for title and contents, and place labels above each of them. Below the labels and text fields, add a rounded rectangle button,

---

setting its text to "Save" (see Figure 5-1). Create outlets for the text fields and button named NoteTitle, NoteContents, and SaveNote. Open *AddNoteViewController.cs* and update it according to Example 5-5:

Example 5-5. AddNoteViewController.cs

```
using MonoTouch.UIKit;

namespace Chapter5.MonoTouchApp
{
    public partial class AddNoteViewController : UIViewController
    {
        public AddNoteViewController()
            : base ("AddNoteViewController", null)
        {
        }

        public override void ViewDidLoad()
        {
            base.ViewDidLoad ();

            Title = "Add Note";

            NoteTitle.ShouldReturn = ❶
                (textField) =>
                {
                    NoteContents.BecomeFirstResponder();

                    return true;
                };

            NoteContents.ShouldReturn = ❷
                (textField) =>
                {
                    textField.ResignFirstResponder();

                    return true;
                };

            SaveNote.TouchUpInside += delegate ❸
            {
                AppDelegate.NoteRepository.Add(
                    NoteTitle.Text, NoteContents.Text);

                NavigationController.PopViewControllerAnimated(true);
            };
        }
    }
}
```

❶ When the user says they are done editing the note's title, automatically move the cursor to edit the note's contents.

❷ Once the user is done editing the note's contents, remove focus from the text field so that the keyboard is hidden.

❸ When the save button is tapped, store the note using the repository and return the user to the list of saved notes.

The last remaining view in the application is the list of saved notes. Add a new class to the project named NoteListViewController, updating it according to Example 5-6:

Example 5-6. NoteListViewController.cs

```
using MonoTouch.UIKit;

namespace Chapter5.MonoTouchApp
{
    public class NoteListViewController : UITableViewController
    {
        public override void ViewDidLoad()
        {
            base.ViewDidLoad ();

            Title = "Notes";

            var addNoteButton = ❶
                new UIBarButtonItem(UIBarButtonSystemItem.Add,
                                    delegate
                                    {
                                        NavigationController.PushViewController(
                                            new AddNoteViewController(), true);
                                    });

            NavigationItem.RightBarButtonItem = addNoteButton;
        }

        public override void ViewDidAppear(bool animated) ❷
        {
            base.ViewDidAppear (animated);

            var notes = AppDelegate.NoteRepository.GetAllNotes();

            TableView.Source = new NoteListTableViewSource(this, notes);
            TableView.ReloadData();
        }
    }
}
```

❶ Add a button to the upper right corner of the view that brings the user to the screen to create a new note.

❷ Every time the view is being shown, update the list from the database. ViewDidAppear() is used instead of ViewDidLoad() in order to catch updates when navigating back to the list after creating or deleting a note, since it will be called each time.

Just as in the application from Chapter 4, the table uses a subclass of UITableViewSource to tell it how to display and behave. Add a new class named NoteListTableViewSource that looks like Example 5-7 to the project.

Example 5-7. NoteListTableViewSource.cs

```
using System.Collections.Generic;
using MonoTouch.Foundation;
using MonoTouch.UIKit;

namespace Chapter5.MonoTouchApp
{
    public class NoteListTableViewSource : UITableViewSource
    {
        private readonly IList<Note> _notes;
        private readonly UIViewController _controller;
        private const string NoteCell = "NoteCell";

        public NoteListTableViewSource(UIViewController controller, IList<Note> notes)
        {
            _controller = controller;
            _notes = notes;
        }

        public override int RowsInSection(UITableView tableview, int section)
        {
            return _notes.Count;
        }

        public override float GetHeightForRow(UITableView tableView, NSIndexPath indexPath)
        {
            return 60;
        }

        public override UITableViewCell GetCell(UITableView tableView, NSIndexPath
indexPath)
        {
            var cell = tableView.DequeueReusableCell(NoteCell)
                    ?? new UITableViewCell(UITableViewCellStyle.Default, NoteCell);
            var note = _notes[indexPath.Row];

            cell.TextLabel.Text = note.Title;

            return cell;
        }

        public override void RowSelected(UITableView tableView, NSIndexPath indexPath)
        {
            var note = _notes[indexPath.Row];

            _controller.NavigationController.PushViewController(
                new ViewNoteViewController(note), true);
        }

        public override void CommitEditingStyle(
```

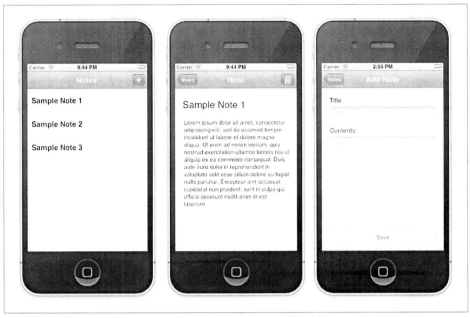

Figure 5-1. Notes application on iOS

```
            UITableView tableView, UITableViewCellEditingStyle editingStyle, NSIndexPath
    indexPath)
        {
            if (editingStyle == UITableViewCellEditingStyle.Delete)
            {
                var note = _notes[indexPath.Row];

                AppDelegate.NoteRepository.Delete(note.Id);

                _notes.Remove(note);

                tableView.DeleteRows(new[] { indexPath }, UITableViewRowAnimation.Fade);
            }
        }
    }
}
```

Most of what is in this class should look very familiar to what you wrote in Chapter 4, with one notable exception. A common convention in iOS lists, when dealing with user-editable data, is for a horizontal swipe on a list item to expose a button to delete the item. In order to follow with platform conventions, this application will implement the same behavior. By overriding the CommitEditingStyle() method in UITableViewSource, you enable this functionality and can hook into the time at which the delete button is tapped. When it is, the note will be deleted via the repository, and the item is removed from the list using a fade animation.

Android

Next, we'll set up the Android application. Create a new Mono for Android application project named Chapter5.MonoAndroidApp. Add the SharedLibrary.MonoAndroid project to the solution, and add a reference to it from Chapter5.MonoAndroidApp. You can remove the activities and layout resources that were added automatically by the template.

When building the iOS app, we added a globally available instance of INoteRepository to the main application class, which can be used throughout the rest of the app. For the Android app, we can do the same thing. Android provides a class, appropriately named Application, that you can subclass in order to help maintain global application information. Any Android app can have at most one Application class, and it gets registered in *AndroidManifest.xml* like any other component. Just as with activities, Mono for Android provides an attribute you can use to decorate the class in order to generate the manifest entry for you automatically.

Create a new class named NoteApplication, modifying it to look like Example 5-8. One important thing to note here is the constructor. In most cases, Mono for Android is able to hide away its interface with the Java side, but this is one exception to that. When subclassing Application, you must make sure to include this call to the base constructor or you will run into issues when trying to run the app.

Example 5-8. NoteApplication.cs

```
using System;
using Android.App;
using Android.Runtime;
using SharedLibrary.Chapter5;

namespace Chapter5.MonoAndroidApp
{
    [Application]
    public class NoteApplication : Application
    {
        public static INoteRepository NoteRepository { get; private set; }

        public NoteApplication(IntPtr javaReference, JniHandleOwnership transfer)
            : base(javaReference, transfer)
        {
        }

        public override void OnCreate()
        {
            base.OnCreate();

            //NoteRepository = new AdoNoteRepository();
            NoteRepository = new XmlNoteRepository();
            NoteRepository.Add("Test", "Post");
        }
    }
}
```

Now you can start defining the screens of the application, starting with the view of a single note. In the *Resources/Layout* folder, add a new Android layout file named *ViewNote.axml*, containing two `TextView` elements to hold the note's title and contents (see Example 5-9). In Android applications, options for user actions are often exposed through a menu that pops up from the bottom when the user taps the device's menu button. This view will follow that convention, putting the delete action in this menu. Inside the *Resources* folder, create a new folder named *Menu*, which as the name implies, will contain any menu definitions needed throughout the application. Add a new XML file named *ViewNote.xml* to this new folder, updating it according to Example 5-10.

Example 5-9. ViewNote.axml

```
<?xml version="1.0" encoding="utf-8"?>
<LinearLayout xmlns:android="http://schemas.android.com/apk/res/android"
    android:orientation="vertical"
    android:layout_width="fill_parent"
    android:layout_height="fill_parent">
    <TextView
        android:id="@+id/Title"
        android:layout_width="match_parent"
        android:layout_height="wrap_content"
        android:textAppearance="?android:attr/textAppearanceLarge"
        android:paddingBottom="5dip"/>

    <TextView
        android:id="@+id/Contents"
        android:layout_width="match_parent"
        android:layout_height="wrap_content" />
</LinearLayout>
```

Example 5-10. ViewNote.xml

```
<?xml version="1.0" encoding="utf-8" ?>
<menu xmlns:android="http://schemas.android.com/apk/res/android">
    <item android:id="@+id/Delete"
        android:title="Delete"/>
</menu>
```

Add a new activity to the project named `ViewNoteActivity` (see Example 5-11). This activity will read in all the details of a note from the `Intent` used to start it. Another option is to simply pass in the ID of the note, and this activity can then look it up. Since the structure of the note is very simple, passing in its details this way avoids an unnecessary trip to the data store to pull out the object. This view will also use the menu defined previously to allow the user to delete the current note.

Example 5-11. ViewNoteActivity.cs

```
using Android.App;
using Android.OS;
using Android.Views;
using Android.Widget;
```

```
namespace Chapter5.MonoAndroidApp
{
    [Activity(Label = "Note")]
    public class ViewNoteActivity : Activity
    {
        private long _noteId;

        protected override void OnCreate(Bundle bundle)
        {
            base.OnCreate(bundle);

            SetContentView(Resource.Layout.ViewNote);

            _noteId = Intent.GetLongExtra("Id", -1); ❶

            FindViewById<TextView>(Resource.Id.Title).Text =
                Intent.GetStringExtra("Title"); ❷
            FindViewById<TextView>(Resource.Id.Contents).Text =
                Intent.GetStringExtra("Contents"); ❸
        }

        public override bool OnCreateOptionsMenu(IMenu menu) ❹
        {
            MenuInflater.Inflate(Resource.Menu.ViewNote, menu);

            return base.OnPrepareOptionsMenu(menu);
        }

        public override bool OnOptionsItemSelected(IMenuItem item) ❺
        {
            if (item.ItemId == Resource.Id.Delete)
            {
                NoteApplication.NoteRepository.Delete(_noteId);

                Finish(); ❻
            }

            return base.OnOptionsItemSelected(item);
        }
    }
}
```

❶ Store the note's ID in case the user wants to delete it later.

❷ Display the note's title in the view.

❸ Display the note's contents in the view.

❹ The OnCreateOptionsMenu() method is called the first time the user clicks the menu button on the device. When this happens, the activity will inflate the menu based on *ViewNote.xml*.

❺ When an item in the options menu is selected, the `OnOptionsItemSelected()` method is called. When the user selects the delete option, the note is deleted using the repository.

❻ Once the note is deleted there is no reason to continue to display it. Calling `Finish()` will dispose of the current activity and return to the previous one in the stack.

Add a new Android layout file to the *Resources/Layout* folder named *AddNote.axml*. In this view, add two `EditText` elements so the user can enter the details for a note, and a `Button` element to click when the user wants to save the note (see Example 5-12). Next, add a new activity to the project named `AddNoteActivity`. This uses this new layout and saves the note when the button is clicked (see Example 5-13).

Example 5-12. AddNote.axml

```
<?xml version="1.0" encoding="utf-8"?>
<LinearLayout xmlns:android="http://schemas.android.com/apk/res/android"
    android:orientation="vertical"
    android:layout_width="fill_parent"
    android:layout_height="fill_parent">
    <TextView
        android:text="Title:"
        android:layout_width="match_parent"
        android:layout_height="wrap_content" />
    <EditText
        android:id="@+id/Title"
        android:layout_width="match_parent"
        android:layout_height="wrap_content" />

    <TextView
        android:text="Contents:"
        android:layout_width="match_parent"
        android:layout_height="wrap_content" />
    <EditText
        android:id="@+id/Contents"
        android:layout_width="match_parent"
        android:layout_height="wrap_content"
        android:singleLine="false"/>

    <Button
        android:id="@+id/Save"
        android:layout_width="match_parent"
        android:layout_height="wrap_content"
        android:text="Save"
        android:paddingTop="10dip"/>
</LinearLayout>
```

Example 5-13. AddNoteActivity.cs

```
using Android.App;
using Android.OS;
using Android.Widget;
```

```
namespace Chapter5.MonoAndroidApp
{
    [Activity(Label = "Add Note")]
    public class AddNoteActivity : Activity
    {
        protected override void OnCreate(Bundle bundle)
        {
            base.OnCreate(bundle);

            SetContentView(Resource.Layout.AddNote);

            FindViewById<Button>(Resource.Id.Save).Click +=
                delegate
                {
                    NoteApplication.NoteRepository.Add(
                        FindViewById<EditText>(Resource.Id.Title).Text,
                        FindViewById<EditText>(Resource.Id.Contents).Text);

                    Finish();
                };
        }
    }
}
```

The last screen of the application will display all of the saved notes and allow the user to view them or add a new one. The process of defining this list will be very similar to the list of tweets in Chapter 4. First, add a new layout file named *Notes.axml* that will contain a single ListView element (see Example 5-14). Add another layout file, this time naming it *NoteListItem.axml*, which will represent a single item in the list. For each item, all we need to display is the note's title, so it should just contain a single TextView element (see Example 5-15). Just as in the view for showing a note, this activity will expose a button to add a new note in the options menu. Add a new XML file named *Notes.xml* to the *Resources/Menu* folder that includes this option (see Example 5-16).

Example 5-14. Notes.axml

```
<?xml version="1.0" encoding="utf-8"?>
<LinearLayout xmlns:android="http://schemas.android.com/apk/res/android"
    android:orientation="vertical"
    android:layout_width="fill_parent"
    android:layout_height="fill_parent">
    <ListView
        android:id="@+id/Notes"
        android:layout_width="match_parent"
        android:layout_height="wrap_content" />
</LinearLayout>
```

Example 5-15. NoteListItem.axml

```
<?xml version="1.0" encoding="utf-8"?>
<LinearLayout xmlns:android="http://schemas.android.com/apk/res/android"
    android:orientation="vertical"
    android:layout_width="fill_parent"
    android:layout_height="fill_parent">
```

```
        <TextView
            android:id="@+id/Title"
            android:layout_width="match_parent"
            android:layout_height="wrap_content"
            android:textAppearance="?android:attr/textAppearanceMedium"
            android:padding="10dip" />
</LinearLayout>
```

Example 5-16. Notes.xml

```
<?xml version="1.0" encoding="utf-8" ?>
<menu xmlns:android="http://schemas.android.com/apk/res/android">
    <item android:id="@+id/Add"
          android:title="Add"/>
</menu>
```

If you recall from Chapter 4, in order to tell a list how to display its contents, you need to provide it with an adapter. Create a new class named NoteListAdapter that will construct the list items based on a list of Notes (see Example 5-17). This should look familiar to what you implemented in Chapter 4, so refer back to that example if you need a reminder on how list adapters work. Now add a new activity named NotesActivity to the project, implementing it according to Example 5-18.

Example 5-17. NoteListAdapter.cs

```
using System.Collections.Generic;
using Android.App;
using Android.Views;
using Android.Widget;
using SharedLibrary.Chapter5;

namespace Chapter5.MonoAndroidApp
{
    public class NoteListAdapter : BaseAdapter<Note>
    {
        private readonly Activity _context;
        private readonly IList<Note> _notes;

        public NoteListAdapter(Activity context, IList<Note> notes)
        {
            _context = context;
            _notes = notes;
        }

        public override long GetItemId(int position)
        {
            return _notes[position].Id;
        }

        public override View GetView(int position, View convertView, ViewGroup parent)
        {
            var view = convertView
                    ?? _context.LayoutInflater.Inflate(Resource.Layout.NoteListItem, null);
```

```
            view.FindViewById<TextView>(Resource.Id.Title).Text = _notes[position].Title;

            return view;
        }

        public override int Count
        {
            get { return _notes == null ? 0 : _notes.Count; }
        }

        public override Note this[int position]
        {
            get { return _notes[position]; }
        }
    }
}
```

Example 5-18. NotesActivity.cs

```
using System.Collections.Generic;
using Android.App;
using Android.Content;
using Android.OS;
using Android.Views;
using Android.Widget;
using SharedLibrary.Chapter5;

namespace Chapter5.MonoAndroidApp
{
    [Activity(Label = "Notes", MainLauncher = true, Icon = "@drawable/icon")]
    public class NotesActivity : Activity
    {
        private ListView _noteList;
        private IList<Note> _notes;

        protected override void OnCreate(Bundle bundle)
        {
            base.OnCreate(bundle);

            SetContentView(Resource.Layout.Notes);

            _noteList = FindViewById<ListView>(Resource.Id.Notes);
            _noteList.ItemClick += (sender, args) => ❶
            {
                var note = _notes[args.Position];

                var intent = new Intent(this, typeof (ViewNoteActivity));
                intent.PutExtra("Id", note.Id);
                intent.PutExtra("Title", note.Title);
                intent.PutExtra("Contents", note.Contents);

                StartActivity(intent);
            };
        }

        protected override void OnResume() ❷
```

```
    {
        base.OnResume();

        _notes = NoteApplication.NoteRepository.GetAllNotes();
        _noteList.Adapter = new NoteListAdapter(this, _notes);
    }

    public override bool OnCreateOptionsMenu(IMenu menu) ❸
    {
        MenuInflater.Inflate(Resource.Menu.Notes, menu);

        return base.OnPrepareOptionsMenu(menu);
    }

    public override bool OnOptionsItemSelected(IMenuItem item) ❹
    {
        if (item.ItemId == Resource.Id.Add)
        {
            StartActivity(typeof(AddNoteActivity));

            return true;
        }

        return base.OnOptionsItemSelected(item);
    }
    }
}
```

❶ When an item in the list is selected, start a new instance of ViewNoteActivity, passing in the note's details.

❷ Update the list of notes in OnResume(), so that it will be called each time the activity is shown. This makes sure the list updates when navigating back from one of the other activities.

❸ Create the options menu for this activity.

❹ When the user clicks the option to add a note, navigate to AddNoteActivity.

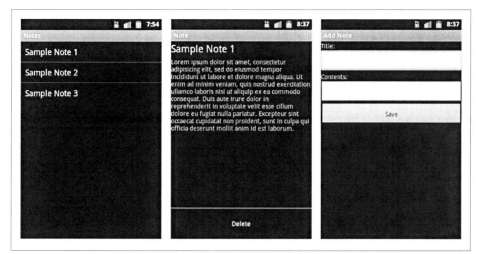

Figure 5-2. Notes application on Android

Windows Phone

Create a new Windows Phone application project named `Chapter5.WindowsPhoneApp`. Add the `SharedLibrary.WindowsPhone` project to the solution, and add a reference to it from `Chapter5.WindowsPhoneApp`.

Open up *App.xaml.cs* and add a public `INoteRepository` property that will be used by the rest of the application (see Example 5-19). In each of the other two applications so far in this chapter, the platform has exposed its own way of presenting action options to the user. Windows Phone is no different. Views in Windows Phone can make use of what is called the *application bar*, where you can place icons and menu items that relate to that view. This bar is shown along the bottom of the screen when in portrait mode, and moves to the side when in landscape mode. The Windows Phone SDK comes with some standard icons that can be used for the application bar, but you're free to use whatever images make sense for your applications. The path to these icons may vary depending on where you installed the SDK to, but it should look similar to:

C:\Program Files (x86)\Microsoft SDKs\Windows Phone\v7.0\Icons\dark

From this folder, copy *appbar.add.rest.png* and *appbar.delete.rest.png* into the project. Make sure to set their Build Action to Content so that you can use them in the application. Now you can create the page for displaying a note to the user. Add a new Windows Phone Portrait Page to the project named *ViewNote.axml*, updating it to look like Example 5-20.

Example 5-19. App.xaml.cs

```
using System.Windows;
using System.Windows.Navigation;
```

```
using Microsoft.Phone.Controls;
using Microsoft.Phone.Shell;
using SharedLibrary.Chapter5;

namespace Chapter5.WindowsPhoneApp
{
    public partial class App : Application
    {
        public static INoteRepository NoteRepository { get; private set; }

        // ...rest of class...
    }
}
```

Example 5-20. ViewNote.xaml

```
<phone:PhoneApplicationPage
    x:Class="Chapter5.WindowsPhoneApp.ViewNote"
    xmlns="http://schemas.microsoft.com/winfx/2006/xaml/presentation"
    xmlns:x="http://schemas.microsoft.com/winfx/2006/xaml"
    xmlns:phone="clr-namespace:Microsoft.Phone.Controls;assembly=Microsoft.Phone"
    xmlns:shell="clr-namespace:Microsoft.Phone.Shell;assembly=Microsoft.Phone"
    xmlns:d="http://schemas.microsoft.com/expression/blend/2008"
    xmlns:mc="http://schemas.openxmlformats.org/markup-compatibility/2006"
    FontFamily="{StaticResource PhoneFontFamilyNormal}"
    FontSize="{StaticResource PhoneFontSizeNormal}"
    Foreground="{StaticResource PhoneForegroundBrush}"
    SupportedOrientations="Portrait" Orientation="Portrait"
    mc:Ignorable="d" d:DesignHeight="696" d:DesignWidth="480"
    shell:SystemTray.IsVisible="True">

    <Grid x:Name="LayoutRoot" Background="Transparent">
        <Grid.RowDefinitions>
            <RowDefinition Height="Auto"/>
            <RowDefinition Height="*"/>
        </Grid.RowDefinitions>

        <StackPanel x:Name="TitlePanel" Grid.Row="0" Margin="12,17,0,28">
            <TextBlock x:Name="ApplicationTitle" Text="Chapter 5" Style="{StaticResource
PhoneTextNormalStyle}"/>
            <TextBlock x:Name="PageTitle" Margin="9,-7,0,0" Style="{StaticResource
PhoneTextTitle1Style}"/>
        </StackPanel>

        <Grid x:Name="ContentPanel" Grid.Row="1" Margin="12,0,12,0">
            <StackPanel Margin="15">
                <TextBlock x:Name="Content" /> ❶
            </StackPanel>
        </Grid>
    </Grid>

    <phone:PhoneApplicationPage.ApplicationBar> ❷
        <shell:ApplicationBar IsVisible="True" IsMenuEnabled="True">
          <shell:ApplicationBarIconButton Text="Delete" IconUri="/appbar.delete.rest.png"
Click="DeleteNote" /> ❸
        </shell:ApplicationBar>
```

```
    </phone:PhoneApplicationPage.ApplicationBar>

</phone:PhoneApplicationPage>
```

❶ Add a TextBlock to contain the note's contents.

❷ Include an application bar in this page.

❸ Add a button to the application bar to alow the user to delete the note, using the delete icon.

Next, open up the page's code-behind file, *ViewNote.xaml.cs*. When the page is loaded it should pull the details of the note out of the query string and display it in the view, saving the ID in case the user wants to delete the note. When the delete button is clicked, use the repository to remove the note and return to the previous page (see Example 5-21).

Example 5-21. ViewNote.xaml.cs

```
using System;
using Microsoft.Phone.Controls;

namespace Chapter5.WindowsPhoneApp
{
    public partial class ViewNote : PhoneApplicationPage
    {
        private int _noteId;

        public ViewNote()
        {
            InitializeComponent();
        }

        protected override void OnNavigatedTo(System.Windows.Navigation.NavigationEventArgs
e)
        {
            base.OnNavigatedTo(e);

            PageTitle.Text = NavigationContext.QueryString["Title"];
            Content.Text = NavigationContext.QueryString["Content"];

            _noteId = int.Parse(NavigationContext.QueryString["Id"]);
        }

        private void DeleteNote(object sender, EventArgs e)
        {
            App.NoteRepository.Delete(_noteId);

            NavigationService.GoBack();
        }
    }
}
```

The second screen of the application will let the user create a new note and save it. Add a new Windows Phone Portrait Page to the project named *AddNote.axml*, updating it to look like Example 5-22.

Example 5-22. AddNote.xaml

```
<phone:PhoneApplicationPage
    x:Class="Chapter5.WindowsPhoneApp.AddNote"
    xmlns="http://schemas.microsoft.com/winfx/2006/xaml/presentation"
    xmlns:x="http://schemas.microsoft.com/winfx/2006/xaml"
    xmlns:phone="clr-namespace:Microsoft.Phone.Controls;assembly=Microsoft.Phone"
    xmlns:shell="clr-namespace:Microsoft.Phone.Shell;assembly=Microsoft.Phone"
    xmlns:d="http://schemas.microsoft.com/expression/blend/2008"
    xmlns:mc="http://schemas.openxmlformats.org/markup-compatibility/2006"
    FontFamily="{StaticResource PhoneFontFamilyNormal}"
    FontSize="{StaticResource PhoneFontSizeNormal}"
    Foreground="{StaticResource PhoneForegroundBrush}"
    SupportedOrientations="Portrait" Orientation="Portrait"
    mc:Ignorable="d" d:DesignHeight="768" d:DesignWidth="480"
    shell:SystemTray.IsVisible="True">

    <Grid x:Name="LayoutRoot" Background="Transparent">
        <Grid.RowDefinitions>
            <RowDefinition Height="Auto"/>
            <RowDefinition Height="*"/>
        </Grid.RowDefinitions>

        <StackPanel x:Name="TitlePanel" Grid.Row="0" Margin="12,17,0,28">
            <TextBlock x:Name="ApplicationTitle" Text="Chapter 5" Style="{StaticResource
PhoneTextNormalStyle}"/>
            <TextBlock x:Name="PageTitle" Text="add note" Margin="9,-7,0,0"
Style="{StaticResource PhoneTextTitle1Style}"/>
        </StackPanel>

        <Grid x:Name="ContentPanel" Grid.Row="1" Margin="12,0,12,0">
            <StackPanel Margin="15">
                <TextBlock Text="Title:" />
                <TextBox x:Name="Title" /> ❶

                <TextBlock Text="Content:" />
                <TextBox x:Name="Content" AcceptsReturn="True" TextWrapping="Wrap" /> ❷

                <Button Click="SaveNote"> ❸
                    <Button.Content>
                        <TextBlock>Save</TextBlock>
                    </Button.Content>
                </Button>
            </StackPanel>
        </Grid>
    </Grid>
</phone:PhoneApplicationPage>
```

❶ Use a TextBlock to accept user input for the note's title.

❷ Use another TextBlock to take user input for the note's contents.

❸ Add a Button that will save the note when clicked.å

Open *AddNote.xaml.cs*, this page's code-behind file. When the save button is clicked, add the note to the data store using the repository and then return the user to the previous page (see Example 5-23).

Example 5-23. AddNote.xaml.cs

```
using System.Windows;
using Microsoft.Phone.Controls;

namespace Chapter5.WindowsPhoneApp
{
    public partial class AddNote : PhoneApplicationPage
    {
        public AddNote()
        {
            InitializeComponent();
        }

        private void SaveNote(object sender, RoutedEventArgs e)
        {
            App.NoteRepository.Add(Title.Text, Content.Text);

            NavigationService.GoBack();
        }
    }
}
```

Last but not least, open up *MainPage.xaml* to create the last screen of the application: the list of saved notes. The layout for this view is very similar to the one in Chapter 4, so you can implement it the same way. In addition, this page will also include an application bar that contains a button to add a note (see Example 5-24). Once that is set up, open the page's code-behind file, *MainPage.xaml.cs*, updating it to look like Example 5-25.

Example 5-24. MainPage.xaml

```
<phone:PhoneApplicationPage
    x:Class="Chapter5.WindowsPhoneApp.MainPage"
    xmlns="http://schemas.microsoft.com/winfx/2006/xaml/presentation"
    xmlns:x="http://schemas.microsoft.com/winfx/2006/xaml"
    xmlns:phone="clr-namespace:Microsoft.Phone.Controls;assembly=Microsoft.Phone"
    xmlns:shell="clr-namespace:Microsoft.Phone.Shell;assembly=Microsoft.Phone"
    xmlns:d="http://schemas.microsoft.com/expression/blend/2008"
    xmlns:mc="http://schemas.openxmlformats.org/markup-compatibility/2006"
    mc:Ignorable="d" d:DesignWidth="480" d:DesignHeight="696"
    FontFamily="{StaticResource PhoneFontFamilyNormal}"
    FontSize="{StaticResource PhoneFontSizeNormal}"
    Foreground="{StaticResource PhoneForegroundBrush}"
    SupportedOrientations="Portrait" Orientation="Portrait"
    shell:SystemTray.IsVisible="True">

    <Grid x:Name="LayoutRoot" Background="Transparent">
```

```xml
        <Grid.RowDefinitions>
            <RowDefinition Height="Auto"/>
            <RowDefinition Height="*"/>
        </Grid.RowDefinitions>

        <StackPanel x:Name="TitlePanel" Grid.Row="0" Margin="12,17,0,28">
            <TextBlock x:Name="ApplicationTitle" Text="Chapter 5" Style="{StaticResource
PhoneTextNormalStyle}"/>
            <TextBlock x:Name="PageTitle" Text="notes" Margin="9,-7,0,0"
Style="{StaticResource PhoneTextTitle1Style}"/>
        </StackPanel>

        <Grid x:Name="ContentPanel" Grid.Row="1" Margin="12,0,12,0">
            <ListBox x:Name="Items" Margin="0,0,-12,0" ItemsSource="{Binding}"
SelectionChanged="NoteSelected">
                <ListBox.ItemTemplate>
                    <DataTemplate>
                        <StackPanel Margin="0,15,0,15">
                            <TextBlock Text="{Binding Title}" Style="{StaticResource
PhoneTextNormalStyle}"/>
                        </StackPanel>
                    </DataTemplate>
                </ListBox.ItemTemplate>
            </ListBox>
        </Grid>
    </Grid>

    <phone:PhoneApplicationPage.ApplicationBar>
        <shell:ApplicationBar IsVisible="True" IsMenuEnabled="True">
            <shell:ApplicationBarIconButton Text="Add" IconUri="/appbar.add.rest.png"
Click="AddNote" />
        </shell:ApplicationBar>
    </phone:PhoneApplicationPage.ApplicationBar>

</phone:PhoneApplicationPage>
```

Example 5-25. MainPage.xaml.cs

```csharp
using System;
using System.Net;
using System.Windows.Controls;
using Microsoft.Phone.Controls;
using SharedLibrary.Chapter5;

namespace Chapter5.WindowsPhoneApp
{
    public partial class MainPage : PhoneApplicationPage
    {
        public MainPage()
        {
            InitializeComponent();
        }

        protected override void OnNavigatedTo(System.Windows.Navigation.NavigationEventArgs
e)
        {
```

```
        base.OnNavigatedTo(e);

        DataContext = null; ❶
        DataContext = App.NoteRepository.GetAllNotes();
    }

    private void NoteSelected(object sender, SelectionChangedEventArgs e)
    {
        if (e.AddedItems.Count == 0) ❷
            return;

        var note = (Note)e.AddedItems[0];

        NavigationService.Navigate( ❸
            new Uri(
                string.Format("/ViewNote.xaml?Id={0}&Title={1}&Content={2}",
                            HttpUtility.UrlEncode(note.Id.ToString()),
                            HttpUtility.UrlEncode(note.Title),
                            HttpUtility.UrlEncode(note.Contents)),
                UriKind.Relative));
    }

    private void AddNote(object sender, EventArgs e)
    {
        NavigationService.Navigate( ❹
            new Uri("/AddNote.xaml", UriKind.Relative));
    }
  }
}
```

❶ When navigating to the page, clear out the DataContext and reset it to the current list of notes. This method will be called even when navigating back to this page from another page.

❷ When navigating back from another page, it's possible for the NoteSelected() method to be fired again with an empty selection. This scenario should be ignored, so this check will make sure that happens.

❸ When a note is selected, navigate to *ViewNote.xaml*, passing in the note's details in the query string.

❹ When the add button is clicked, navigate to *AddNote.xaml*.

Accessing the Filesystem

Now that the applications for all three platforms are ready to go, it's time to look at some options for implementing INoteRepository to actually store and retrieve the data. One thing to note here is how far you were able to get before having to actually provide this implementation. By applying the abstraction pattern introduced in Chapter 3, the applications were able to work against the interface instead of worrying about the implementation details.

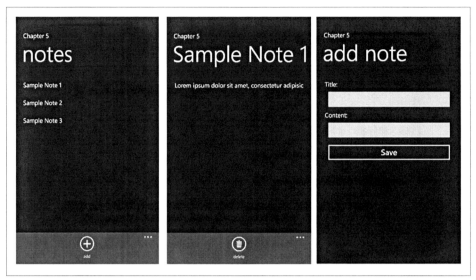

Figure 5-3. Notes application on Windows Phone

Direct File Access

The first option for persisting data is to simply write to and read from files on the device. The .NET Base Class Library provides a rich set of classes for accessing files, directories, and data streams, which are mostly found in the System.IO namespace. Both iOS and Android give you direct access to the filesystem, meaning that you can access files the same way you would on a computer, using the same System.IO classes. Example 5-26 shows some examples of using some System.IO classes to read and write files, but is by no means exhaustive, as the Base Class Library includes an extensive set of classes you can leverage.

Example 5-26. Accessing a file directly

```
// 1) writing to a file using convenience method on File
File.WriteAllText("/path/to/file", "Foo, bar, baz.");

// 2) writing to a file using a stream
using (var writer = new StreamWriter("/path/to/file"))
{
    writer.WriteLine("Foo, bar, baz.");
}

// 3) reading from a file using convenience method on File
string fileContents = File.ReadAllText("/path/to/file");

// 4) reading from a file using a stream
using (var reader = new StreamReader("/path/to/file"))
{
    fileContents = reader.ReadToEnd();
}
```

iOS

Although both provide direct filesystem access, each platform has its own folder paths and conventions to follow. On iOS, each application's files are sandboxed to that application, so they are not accessible to any other application on the device. Within every application's sandbox, iOS provides the following folders for storing data, each with its own purpose and behavior:

Documents
> This folder is used to store documents created by the user, and will be backed up by iTunes. You can get the path to this folder by calling `Environment.GetFolderPath` `(Environment.SpecialFolder.Personal)`

Library
> This folder is used to store application data that was not created by the user, such as a database, and will be backed up by iTunes.

Library/Preferences
> Application preferences are saved to this folder, and are backed up by iTunes.

Library/Caches
> Use this folder to store cached data used by your application. The contents of this folder should not be required for the application run, and should simply enhance it. This folder is not backed up by iTunes.

tmp
> Use this folder to store temporary files that have a short lifespan. If you use this folder, take care to clean up files once they are no longer needed in order to free up space. In some cases the OS may clean out files in this folder on its own as well to reclaim space. This folder is not backed up by iTunes.

All of these folders are created under the application's root folder. You can get the path of the root folder by going up one directory from Documents:

Example 5-27. Getting the root directory of an iOS app

```
string root = Path.Combine(
            Environment.GetFolderPath(Environment.SpecialFolder.Personal),
            "..")
```

Android

In Android, the two main types of file storage you can access are categorized as internal storage and external storage. Internal storage refers to the device's internal, non-removable memory. Just like iOS, an application's files are private to that application, so they cannot be read from other applications on the device. Unlike iOS, Android doesn't break down the folder structure into many different subfolders, instead providing two main places for you to store files:

Application folder

> This is the folder created in the device's internal memory for you to store data. You can get the path to this folder by calling `Environment.GetFolderPath(Environ ment.SpecialFolder.Personal)`

Cache

> This is a folder in internal memory used to save temporary files used by the application. To sure to dispose of files in this folder once they are no longer needed. If Android decides it needs to reclaim space, it may delete files in this folder on its own. The path to this folder is available in an activity through its `CacheDir` property.

Some Android devices also have extra memory, such as an SD card, which is referred to as external storage. Files stored in external storage are considered public, and can be read by other applications as well as the user when he connects the device to his computer. Because of this, you should never use external storage to store private application data.

When working with external storage, you should always be careful to check first that it's there. In some cases, the device may not have any external storage, or it may have been removed. If the user connects the device to the computer and enables USB mass storage in order to view the files, the device will not be able to read from external storage until it is unmounted.

Example 5-28 shows how to check that the external storage is mounted and get the file path for its folder for pictures:

Example 5-28. Accessing external storage in Android

```
if (Android.OS.Environment.ExternalStorageState == Android.OS.Environment.MediaMounted)
{
    string path =
        Android.OS.Environment.GetExternalStoragePublicDirectory(
            Android.OS.Environment.DirectoryPictures).Path;
}
```

There are several standard folders used in external storage for organizing shared data and can be sent into the call to `GetExternalStoragePublicDirectory()`. If the folder does not already exist in external storage, calling this method will also create it. As these folders are considered public, they are not modified or removed when your application is uninstalled, so be sure to only store things there that should remain on the device even if your application is no longer there.

`DirectoryAlarms`

> Contains audio files to include in the list of alarms the user can select from

`DirectoryDcim`

> Location for pictures and videos when the device is mounted as a camera

`DirectoryDownloads`

> Contains files downloaded by the user

DirectoryMovies
> Contains movies available to the user

DirectoryMusic
> Contains music files available to the user

DirectoryNotifications
> Contains audio files to include in the list of notifications the user can select from

DirectoryPictures
> Contains images available to the user

DirectoryPodcasts
> Contains podcasts available to the user

DirectoryRingtones
> Contains audio files to include in the list of ringtones the user can select from

Isolated Storage

Even though direct file access is possible for iOS and Android, Windows Phone doesn't support it. Instead, Windows Phone borrows from Silverlight's methods for file access and makes use of *isolated storage*. Isolated storage provides a layer on top of the operating system's actual filesystem so that it can maintain a higher level of control on how data is stored. The good news here is that both MonoTouch and Mono for Android provide isolated storage APIs that line up directly with Windows Phone, meaning that code designed to use the isolated storage APIs can easily be shared across all platforms.

To demonstrate this, we'll build an INoteRepository implementation that uses reads and writes its data through isolated storage, making use of .NET's built-in XML serialization capabilities along the way. Another option would be to use direct file access on Android and iOS, and isolated storage on Windows Phone, depending on the needs of the application. In this case, using isolated storage allows for complete code reuse of the repository.

Back in the SharedLibrary project, add a new class to the *Chapter5* folder named XmlNoteRepository:

Example 5-29. XmlNoteRepository.cs

```
using System.Collections.Generic;
using System.IO;
using System.IO.IsolatedStorage;
using System.Linq;
using System.Xml.Serialization;

namespace SharedLibrary.Chapter5
{
    public class XmlNoteRepository : INoteRepository
    {
        private const string DatabaseFile = "Notes.db";
        private List<Note> _notes;
```

```csharp
public XmlNoteRepository()
{
    using (var store = IsolatedStorageFile.GetUserStoreForApplication())
    {
        if (!store.FileExists(DatabaseFile)) ❶
        {
            _notes = new List<Note>();
            saveNotesFile();
        }
        else
        {
            loadNotesFromFile();
        }
    }
}

private void loadNotesFromFile() ❷
{
    var serializer = new XmlSerializer(typeof(List<Note>));

    using (var store = IsolatedStorageFile.GetUserStoreForApplication())
    using (var reader = store.OpenFile(DatabaseFile, FileMode.Open))
    {
        _notes = (List<Note>)serializer.Deserialize(reader);
    }
}

private void saveNotesFile() ❸
{
    var serializer = new XmlSerializer(typeof(List<Note>));

    using (var store = IsolatedStorageFile.GetUserStoreForApplication())
    using (var writer = store.OpenFile(DatabaseFile, FileMode.Create))
    {
        serializer.Serialize(writer, _notes);
    }
}

public IList<Note> GetAllNotes() ❹
{
    return _notes;
}

public void Add(string title, string contents) ❺
{
    _notes.Add(
        new Note
        {
            Id = _notes.Count == 0
                    ? 1
                    : _notes.Max(note => note.Id) + 1,
            Title = title,
            Contents = contents
        });
```

```
        saveNotesFile();
    }

    public void Delete(long id) ❻
    {
        _notes = _notes.Where(note => note.Id != id).ToList();

        saveNotesFile();
    }
  }
}
```

❶ When the repository is created, check to see if the file exists in isolated storage. If it doesn't, save an empty list. If it does, load the notes out of the list.

❷ Read the contents of the file and deserialize it into a list of Notes.

❸ Serialize the current list of Notes into XML and write it out to a file, creating the file if it doesn't already exist.

❹ Since the current list is always kept in memory, GetAllNotes() can just return that list.

❺ First, create a new Note object based on the provided title and contents, naively generating its ID based on the current contents of the list. Add that new note to the list, and then refresh the saved copy.

❻ Filter out any Notes in the list that match the given ID and refresh the saved list.

This is admittedly not the most efficient implementation, but you can see how without very much code you can achieve a good level of data persistence that is completely cross-platform ready. In fact, this class can be used as is on iOS, Android, and Windows Phone, so add a link to the file in SharedLibrary.MonoTouch, SharedLibrary.MonoAndroid and SharedLibrary.WindowsPhone.

Now the applications built in the first section can be updated to use this implementation. Since they were built to work against the INoteRepository interface, each application only needs to be changed in one place in order to plug in our implementation. After doing so, you should be able to run the applications and successfully add and remove notes from the data store. Refer to Figure 5-1 (iOS), Figure 5-2 (Android), and Figure 5-3 (Windows Phone) for a reference on what the applications look like in action.

iOS

In Chapter5.MonoTouchApp, open up *AppDelegate.cs* and create the repository inside the FinishedLaunching() method:

Example 5-30. AppDelegate.cs (updates only)

```
public partial class AppDelegate : UIApplicationDelegate
{
    // ...existing code in class...

    public override bool FinishedLaunching(UIApplication app, NSDictionary options)
    {
        NoteRepository = new AdoNoteRepository();

        // ...existing code in method...
    }
}
```

Android

In Chapter5.MonoAndroidApp, modify the NoteApplication class so that it creates the repository inside of the OnCreate() callback:

Example 5-31. NoteApplication.cs (updates only)

```
public class NoteApplication : Application
{
    // ...existing code in class...

    public override void OnCreate()
    {
        base.OnCreate();

        NoteRepository = new XmlNoteRepository();
    }
}
```

Windows Phone

In Chapter5.WindowsPhoneApp, open *App.xaml.cs* and create the repository inside the Application_Launching() method:

Example 5-32. App.xaml.cs (updates only)

```
public partial class App : Application
{
    // ...existing code in class...

    private void Application_Launching(object sender, LaunchingEventArgs e)
    {
        NoteRepository = new XmlNoteRepository();
    }
}
```

Using a Local Database

Storing and retrieving data using the filesystem works well for some scenarios, but there are many cases where you might want to leverage the device's local database to gain access to a more powerful relational data store. The good news is that all three platforms provide local database capabilities. However, unlike the previous example with isolated storage, there's no standardized way to share all database code across all three platforms. That said, it's still possible to achieve some code reuse along the way, as the following example will demonstrate.

When working with databases, it's important to remember the kinds of devices your applications will be running on. For databases used in normal server environments, characteristics like power consumption and processing power are often non-issues, but with mobile devices, they are very significant. Having access to a local database can be a very convenient and powerful tool, but always keep in mind the environment. Even when you're not working with a database, you should always be conscious of this.

iOS and Android

The iOS and Android platforms each make use of SQLite for databases. SQLite is small relational database system that stores all data for a database in a single file, and is designed to be compact and easily embeddable. As a result, SQLite is widely used in many environments outside of mobile devices as well, including most modern web browsers. Since the database file is independent of the system it was created on, this makes it possible to ship your application bundled with an initial database that it can continue to modify after installation.

Both MonoTouch and Mono for Android include an ADO.NET provider for SQLite. ADO.NET is part of .NET's Base Class Library, and includes many classes that can be used when working against relational databases. If you've worked with databases in other .NET projects, you've likely encountered ADO.NET classes before, such as `SqlCommand` and `SqlDataReader`.

Even though the `System.Data` namespace is brought along in MonoTouch and Mono for Android, not all of it can be used on these platforms. Some parts of Mono's ADO.NET provider for SQLite, found in the `Mono.Data.Sqlite` namespace, depend on a newer version of SQLite than is available on both iOS and Android. For the most part, the missing functionality is in features that query the database schema at runtime, such as the `DataTable` class. Even though your code will compile if you use these methods, your application will crash at runtime when you try to invoke them. You will also run into other issues on Android versions earlier than version 2.2 (Froyo), as the SQLite version used prior to that release is missing even more methods needed by `Mono.Data.Sqlite`.

Since MonoTouch and Mono for Android both include bindings to the native database APIs of the platform, you can always drop back to those if you find yourself stuck trying to do something that isn't supported by the ADO.NET provider. This application doesn't need to access any of these unsupported features, which means that all of the database code can be completely reused across both iOS and Android.

In the SharedLibrary project, add a new class named AdoNoteRepository to the *Chapter5* folder:

Example 5-33. AdoNoteRepository.cs

```
#if __ANDROID_8__ || MONOTOUCH ❶
public class AdoNoteRepository : INoteRepository
{
    private readonly string _databasePath;

    public AdoNoteRepository()
    {
        _databasePath = Path.Combine( ❷
                            Environment.GetFolderPath(Environment.SpecialFolder.Personal),
                            "Notes.db");

        setupDatabase(); ❸
    }

    private void setupDatabase()
    {
        using (var connection = getConnection())
        using (var command = connection.CreateCommand())
        {
            if (!File.Exists(_databasePath)) ❹
                SqliteConnection.CreateFile(_databasePath);

            connection.Open();
            command.CommandText = ❺
                @"CREATE TABLE IF NOT EXISTS Notes (
                    Id INTEGER PRIMARY KEY AUTOINCREMENT,
                    Title TEXT NOT NULL,
                    Contents TEXT NOT NULL
                )";

            command.ExecuteNonQuery();
            connection.Close();
        }
    }

    private SqliteConnection getConnection()
    {
        return new SqliteConnection("Data Source=" + _databasePath);
    }

    public IList<Note> GetAllNotes() ❻
    {
        var notes = new List<Note>();

        using (var connection = getConnection())
        using (var command = connection.CreateCommand())
```

```
        {
            connection.Open();
            command.CommandText = "SELECT * FROM Notes";

            using (var reader = command.ExecuteReader())
            {
                while (reader.Read())
                {
                    notes.Add(
                        new Note
                        {
                            Id = (long)reader["Id"],
                            Title = (string)reader["Title"],
                            Contents = (string)reader["Contents"]
                        });
                }
            }

            connection.Close();
        }

        return notes;
    }

    public void Add(string title, string contents) ❼
    {
        using (var connection = getConnection())
        using (var command = connection.CreateCommand())
        {
            connection.Open();

            command.CommandText = "INSERT INTO Notes (Title, Contents) VALUES (@title,
@contents)";
            command.Parameters.AddWithValue("@title", title);
            command.Parameters.AddWithValue("@contents", contents);

            command.ExecuteNonQuery();

            connection.Close();
        }
    }

    public void Delete(long id) ❽
    {
        using (var connection = getConnection())
        using (var command = connection.CreateCommand())
        {
            connection.Open();

            command.CommandText = "DELETE FROM Notes WHERE Id=@id";
            command.Parameters.AddWithValue("@id", id);

            command.ExecuteNonQuery();

            connection.Close();
```

```
        }
      }
    }
#endif
```

❶ Use conditional compilation to make sure this is only compiled for iOS and Android, the platforms that support this method, making sure to require at least API level 8 on Android.

❷ Determine the file path to use for the database file, based on the home directory for the current application.

❸ Make sure the database is set up properly when the repository is created.

❹ If the database file does not exist, create a new SQLite database using that file path.

❺ Create the Notes table in the database if it is not already there.

❻ Read out all rows from the Notes table, constructing and return a list of Note objects using the data returned.

❼ Insert a new row into the Notes table using the provided values.

❽ Delete the row from the Notes table with a matching ID.

You can link this file into all three of the mobile SharedLibrary projects. Since it is not useful for Windows Phone, you have the option of omitting the link from that project, but due to the use of conditional compilation it won't be compiled on that platform either way. As it is useful for both iOS and Android, it makes sense to keep the in SharedLibrary. For both the SharedLibrary.MonoTouch and SharedLibrary.MonoAndroid projects, add references to Mono.Data.Sqlite to make the projects compile properly.

 You may be wondering why, as written, the class will not be compiled for the base SharedLibrary project, which is a standard .NET class library. The SQLite ADO.NET provider is available for the full .NET framework as well, but since that is outside the scope of these examples, it is simpler just to exclude it here. You can download the System.Data.Sqlite provider at *http://system.data.sqlite.org*.

Following the same steps as in the last section, update Chapter5.MonoTouchApp and Chapter5.MonoAndroidApp to create an instance of AdoNoteRepository instead of XmlNoteRepository. When you run the applications, the behavior will be exactly the same, but behind the scenes the data is being persisted to the database, using exactly the same database code.

Windows Phone

Whereas the other platforms use SQLite as the database, Windows Phone makes use of SQL Server Compact Edition (CE) instead. Just as with SQLite, SQL Server CE also stores a database in a single file and is easily redistributable. Since the Windows Phone platform does not allow for accessing the database directly through ADO.NET, it cannot share the same code as iOS and Android. Instead, the Windows Phone database can only be accessed by using its LINQ to SQL API, meaning that is not possible to execute raw SQL queries against the database as in the previous example. While this may sound like a negative thing, this API actually provides a lot of power and flexibility, and is very easy to work with. The database file itself is stored inside of the application's isolated storage, so it is still sandboxed to the application, just as with the other platforms.

 Local database support was added in version 7.1 of the Windows Phone SDK and version 7.5 (Mango) of the operating system. If you are trying to target an earlier version of Windows Phone, your only option is to fall back on using the filesystem.

One of the requirements of using LINQ to SQL is that the model class, Note in this case, needs to be properly annotated using various attributes so that the system knows how to relate it to the underlying database. In the SharedLibrary project, open the Note class and update it according to Example 5-34:

Example 5-34. Note.cs

```
#if WINDOWS_PHONE
    using System.Data.Linq.Mapping;
#endif

#if WINDOWS_PHONE
    [Table]
    public class Note
    {
        [Column(IsDbGenerated = true, IsPrimaryKey = true)]
        public long Id { get; set; }

        [Column]
        public string Title { get; set; }

        [Column]
        public string Contents { get; set; }
    }
#else
    public class Note
    {
        public long Id { get; set; }
        public string Title { get; set; }
        public string Contents { get; set; }
```

```
    }
#endif
```

Since the attributes are only applicable to Windows Phone, conditional compilation is used to make sure the other platforms, do not try to compile them while still allowing both sides to share the same model class. In this example, a separate copy of Note was created for both conditions, but the conditional statements could have just been placed around each attribute as well. Since this class only contains three properties, separating them helps keep the code a little more readable, but either way the result will be identical. The [Table] attribute that decorates the class declaration tells the system that this class corresponds directly to a table in the database. Since each property should be mapped to a column in the table, each is decorated with the [Column] attribute, also specifying that the value for the Id column should be generated automatically by the database when inserting a new record. In both SharedLibrary.WindowsPhone and Chapter5.WindowsPhoneApp, add a reference to System.Data.Linq.

Now that the model is properly annotated, we need to define a DataContext, a proxy for the database that interacts with the LINQ to SQL runtime to perform queries and handle object mappings. In Chapter5.WindowsPhoneApp, create a new class named NoteContext:

Example 5-35. NoteContext.cs

```
public class NoteContext : DataContext
{
    public NoteContext(string connectionString)
        : base(connectionString)
    {
    }

    public Table<Note> Notes
    {
        get { return GetTable<Note>(); }
    }
}
```

Since this application's database only consists of a single table, the data context only needs to declare the one property and pass a connection string to the base class's constructor. This class is what will be used to implement the repository and handle all interactions with the database. Add a new class to Chapter5.WindowsPhoneApp named SqlNoteRepository, modifying it according to Example 5-36:

Example 5-36. SqlNoteRepository.cs

```
public class SqlNoteRepository : INoteRepository
{
    private readonly string _connectionString = "Data Source=isostore:/Notes.sdf"; ❶

    public SqlNoteRepository()
    {
        using (var db = new NoteContext(_connectionString))
```

```
        {
            if (!db.DatabaseExists()) ❷
                db.CreateDatabase();
        }
    }

    public IList<Note> GetAllNotes()
    {
        using (var db = new NoteContext(_connectionString))
        {
            return db.Notes.ToList(); ❸
        }
    }

    public void Add(string title, string contents)
    {
        using (var db = new NoteContext(_connectionString))
        {
            db.Notes.InsertOnSubmit( ❹
                new Note
                {
                    Title = title,
                    Contents = contents
                });
            db.SubmitChanges();
        }
    }

    public void Delete(long id)
    {
        using (var db = new NoteContext(_connectionString))
        {
            var noteToDelete = db.Notes.First(note => note.Id == id); ❺

            db.Notes.DeleteOnSubmit(noteToDelete);
            db.SubmitChanges();
        }
    }
}
```

❶ Set the connection string for the database, which will be stored in the application's isolated storage.

❷ When the repository is created check if the database exists, creating it if it does not.

❸ Use LINQ to SQL to return a list of all Notes in the database.

❹ Create a new Note based on the given data and insert it into the database. Since we specified that the Id property is generated by the database it will be populated automatically when the changes are submitted.

❺ Find the Note with the given ID in the database and delete it.

Now you can update *App.xaml.cs* to create an instance of `SqlNoteRepository` instead of `XmlNoteRepository`. Running the application will show the exact same behavior once again, but this time the data is being stored in the application's local database.

Open Source Alternatives

So far in this chapter, you have seen that the options for using a local database vary across each platform, particularly between the Mono platforms and Windows Phone. There are a couple open source projects that are worth mentioning here, which can be very useful in sharing database code across all three platforms at once.

The first project is **C#-SQLite**, written by Noah Hart. C#-SQLite is a port of the SQLite source code, rewritten in C#. This allows it to be used in .NET applications that may not already be able to use SQLite, such as Silverlight and Windows Phone. You can add this project to your Windows Phone applications to make use of a local SQLite database, regardless of which version of Windows Phone the device is running. More information about C#-SQLite can be found at *http://code.google.com/p/csharp-sqlite*.

The second project worth mentioning here is **sqlite-net**, developed by Frank Krueger. This project acts as a thin layer over a SQLite database, providing methods for executing strongly typed queries against the database. Sqlite-net also acts as a simple *object-relational mapping (ORM)* layer, allowing you to use your existing data model to construct and query the database. It was originally written with MonoTouch in mind, but also works well in Mono for Android applications in addition to other .NET-based environments. By combining this with C#-SQLite, you can also use sqlite-net on Windows Phone, allowing you to share database code across all three platforms. You can find out more about sqlite-net at *http://code.google.com/p/sqlite-net*.

Summary

Over the course of this chapter, we explored different approaches to persisting data in your applications, making use of the local filesystem as well as relational databases. Along the way, we built a complete application for each platform that accepts user input, stores it, and allows the user to view or delete the saved items. In each of them, the options for adding or deleting items were presented according to the standard for that platform, keeping the user experience in line with other apps on the platform. We also explored the differences in what is possible on each platform, and where it is and isn't possible to share code between them. Additionally, we also discussed some open source projects that can help you share more of your application's database code across platforms. Hopefully, at this point you are starting to get an idea of the different pieces that go into putting together apps on the different platforms. In the next chapter, we will start digging into the geolocation and mapping capabilities of each platform.

CHAPTER 6

Location, Location, Location

One of the biggest reasons that smartphones have taken off in recent years is their ability to provide real-time information about what's around you. You can look up restaurants in the area, read reviews about them, browse their menus, and even make a reservation. If you're lost, you can quickly pinpoint your location on a map and get directions to where you need to go. Having access to the user's current location is a very powerful feature, and can allow your application to provide a very personalized and localized experience to the user.

This chapter will introduce the location and mapping capabilities of each platform. Whereas the previous chapters focused largely on sharing code across them, the applications in this chapter will be independent from each other, despite providing the same functionality. That's not to say that there is no potential code reuse in these scenarios, though. If you recall, the example in Chapter 2 demonstrated how you might apply the abstraction pattern to building an application that utilizes the user's location. Since each platform has its own way of doing mapping and location, it makes sense to assess them individually rather than rushing into an abstraction.

The applications in this chapter will be built in two phases. In the first, the user will see a map centered on New York City, where she can zoom and pan around, and where there will be a marker showing the location. The second part of this chapter will expand it to re-center the map according to the user's location, placing a marker there as well. Along the way, you will also see how you can provide fake location data to each of the emulators.

Mapping

iOS

Create a new empty iPhone project named Chapter6.MonoTouchApp. Add a new iPhone View Controller to the project named MapViewController, and then open *MapViewController.xib* in Interface Builder. From the list of views in the toolbox, click and drag a Map View onto the view, sizing it so that it takes up the entire space of the view. Add an outlet for it named Map so it can be accessed from the view controller code. If you need a refresher on how to set up an outlet, refer back to the example in Chapter 2. That's the only thing needed for this application's view, so open up *MapViewController.cs*, updating it according to Example 6-1. Also be sure to update *AppDelegate.cs* to have the application load up this view controller when the app launches, using the same approach as the previous chapters.

Example 6-1. MapViewController.cs

```
using MonoTouch.CoreLocation;
using MonoTouch.MapKit;
using MonoTouch.UIKit;

namespace Chapter6.MonoTouchApp
{
    public partial class MapViewController : UIViewController
    {
        public MapViewController()
            : base ("MapViewController", null)
        {
        }

        public override void ViewDidLoad()
        {
            base.ViewDidLoad ();

            var newYorkCity = new CLLocationCoordinate2D(40.716667, -74); ❶

            Map.CenterCoordinate = newYorkCity; ❷
            Map.Region = MKCoordinateRegion.FromDistance (newYorkCity, 5000, 5000); ❸

            var annotation = new MapAnnotation("New York City", newYorkCity); ❹
            Map.AddAnnotation(annotation);
        }
    }
}
```

❶ Create a `CLLocationCoordinate2D` object that represents New York City's location.

❷ Center the map on that location.

❸ Tell the map to zoom out such that the view is 5000 meters^2 around the center.

❹ Add an annotation to the map, labeling the center as New York City.

In iOS, the location APIs are referred to as *Core Location* and the mapping APIs are part of *Map Kit*, hence the class prefixes of CL and MK. This code also makes use of a `MapAnnotation` class, which has not been defined yet. In order to add an annotation to the map, you must provide a subclass of the abstract `MKAnnotationClass`, which will specify how the annotation will act and where it should go. Add a new class named `MapAnnotation` to the project that simply takes in a title and location of the annotation (see Example 6-2).

That's all the code you need to have basic mapping functionality in your app! If you run the application, now it should look like Figure 6-1. Tapping on the pin will cause the annotation's title to be shown.

Example 6-2. MapAnnotation.cs

```
using MonoTouch.CoreLocation;
using MonoTouch.MapKit;

namespace Chapter6.MonoTouchApp
{
    public class MapAnnotation : MKAnnotation
    {
        private readonly string _title;
        private CLLocationCoordinate2D _coordinate;

        public MapAnnotation(string title, CLLocationCoordinate2D coordinate)
        {
            _title = title;
            _coordinate = coordinate;
        }

        public override CLLocationCoordinate2D Coordinate
        {
            get { return _coordinate; }
            set { _coordinate = value; }
        }

        public override string Title
        {
            get { return _title; }
        }
    }
}
```

Figure 6-1. Map application for iOS

Android

Create a new Mono for Android application project named Chapter6.MonoAndroidApp. As with the other examples in previous chapters, you can remove the activities and layout resources that were added automatically by the project template.

In order to use the Google Maps API in your application you need to add a reference to Mono.Android.GoogleMaps, which comes as part of Mono for Android. Adding this reference will do two things for you in your application. First, it will allow you to access the Google Maps API from C#. Second, it will add the following line to your application's generated *AndroidManifest.xml*:

Example 6-3. AndroidManifest.xml (partial)

```
<uses-library android:name="com.google.android.maps" />
```

Up until now, all the parts of Android we have accessed have been a part of the core Android APIs. Although they are developed and maintained by Google, the Google Maps APIs for Android are part of a separate library rather than Android itself. They are released under different licensing terms than Android; this separation allows vendors to decide for themselves whether they want to include it or not. While it's not mandatory, a vast majority of devices in the market today do include the library, so it's often safe to rely on it. Including this line in *AndroidManifest.xml* will prevent Android from installing the application if the library is not found on the device, and also tells the market to hide the app from users who cannot install it. This restriction applies to the emulator as well, which is why in Chapter 2, we created an emulator image that includes the Google APIs.

Now that the Google Maps API is available to the application, add a new Android layout to the *Resources/Layout* folder named *Map.axml*. This view will contain a single `MapView` element that takes up the entire screen and has an ID of `Map` so it can be accessed from the activity code (see Example 6-4).

 In order to use Google Maps in an Android application, you need to obtain an API key from Google and supply it to the `MapView` instance (see Example 6-4). Registering for an API key is free, and only requires agreeing to Google's Terms of Service. Details on how to obtain a key for your Mono for Android application are available at *http://docs.xa marin.com/android/advanced_topics/Obtaining_a_Google_Maps_API _Key*.

Example 6-4. Map.axml

```
<?xml version="1.0" encoding="utf-8"?>
<LinearLayout xmlns:android="http://schemas.android.com/apk/res/android"
    android:orientation="vertical"
    android:layout_width="fill_parent"
    android:layout_height="fill_parent">
    <com.google.android.maps.MapView
            android:id="@+id/Map"
            android:layout_width="match_parent"
            android:layout_height="match_parent"
            android:enabled="true"
            android:clickable="true"
            android:apiKey="Your Key Goes Here" />
</LinearLayout>
```

The Google Maps API provides an abstract class named `MapActivity` that you can extend, which takes care of most of the work involved in displaying a map to the user. Add a new activity to the project named `LocationActivity` that extends `MapActivity`:

Example 6-5. LocationActivity.cs

```csharp
using Android.App;
using Android.GoogleMaps;
using Android.OS;

namespace Chapter6.MonoAndroidApp
{
    [Activity(Label = "Map", MainLauncher = true, Icon = "@drawable/icon")]
    public class LocationActivity : MapActivity
    {
        private MapOverlay _mapOverlay;
        private MapView _map;

        protected override void OnCreate(Bundle bundle)
        {
            base.OnCreate(bundle);

            SetContentView(Resource.Layout.Map); ❶

            _map = FindViewById<MapView>(Resource.Id.Map); ❷
            _map.SetBuiltInZoomControls(true);

            var newYorkCity = new GeoPoint((int) (40.716667 * 1e6), (int) (-74 * 1e6)); ❸
            _map.Controller.SetCenter(newYorkCity); ❹
            _map.Controller.SetZoom(14); ❺

            _mapOverlay = new MapOverlay(Resources.GetDrawable(Resource.Drawable.Icon),
this); ❻
            _map.Overlays.Add(_mapOverlay); ❼

            _mapOverlay.Add(newYorkCity, "New York City"); ❽
        }

        protected override bool IsRouteDisplayed ❾
        {
            get { return false; }
        }
    }
}
```

❶ Set the view to *Map.axml*.

❷ Get a reference to the map element in the layout, enabling the built-in zoom controls provided by the API.

❸ Create a GeoPoint object representing New York City's location.

❹ Center the map at this location.

❺ Set the map's initial zoom level. A zoom level of 1 means the map is fully zoomed out, with each successive zoom level magnifying the map by a factor of 2.

❻ Create a map overlay using the project's default icon as a marker.

❼ Add the overlay to the map.

❽ Add New York City's location to the overlay so a marker will be displayed on the map.

❾ Specify that this map will not be displaying route information.

Google's Terms of Service for using the Google Maps API requires that you let Google know when your map activity is displaying route information, such as giving the user directions to some destination. Since this application is not doing that, it is safe to return false for the IsRouteDisplayed property.

You may have also noticed some strange looking conversions involved in constructing the GeoPoint object for New York City's location. The GeoPoint class stores its coordinates in microdegrees, so the degrees for latitude and longitude must be multiplied by 100,000 to get the value in microdegrees. In C#, writing 1e6 is shorthand for $1 * 10^6$, or 100,000. They are all equivalent to the compiler, so you are free to use any representation of the number that you want.

In order to show markers on a map, the API provides another abstract class named ItemizedOverlay that you can extend to specify how they should look and behave. You can think of this as a layer of markers that lies on top of the map, containing as many markers as you need. LocationActivity references a class named MapOverlay which has not been created yet. Add a new class named MapOverlay to the project that extends ItemizedOverlay to display a list of points, storing a title for each of them (see Example 6-6).

Example 6-6. MapOverlay.cs

```
using System.Collections.Generic;
using Android.Content;
using Android.GoogleMaps;
using Android.Graphics.Drawables;
using Android.Widget;

namespace Chapter6.MonoAndroidApp
{
    public class MapOverlay : ItemizedOverlay
    {
        private readonly Context _context;
        private readonly IList<OverlayItem> _overlayItems = new List<OverlayItem>(); ❶

        public MapOverlay(Drawable marker, Context context)
            : base(BoundCenterBottom(marker)) ❷
        {
            _context = context;
        }

        public void Add(GeoPoint point, string title) ❸
        {
            _overlayItems.Add(new OverlayItem(point, title, null));

            Populate(); ❹
        }
```

```
protected override Java.Lang.Object CreateItem(int i) ❺
{
    return _overlayItems[i];
}

public override int Size() ❻
{
    return _overlayItems.Count;
}

protected override bool OnTap(int index) ❼
{
    Toast
        .MakeText(_context, _overlayItems[index].Title, ToastLength.Short)
        .Show();

    return base.OnTap(index);
}
    }
}
```

❶ Maintain a list of all overlay items to be displayed.

❷ Require that a drawable be passed in through the constructor that will be used to display each item, instructing the base class to position the item according to the bottom center of the drawable.

❸ Provide a public method for adding a new item to the layer, creating a new `Over layItem` object and adding it to the list.

❹ Calling `Populate()` will tell the base class that it should draw the items on the map.

❺ The `CreateItem()` method is called by `Populate()`, providing it with the item to display.

❻ The `Size()` method is also called by `Populate()`, telling it how many items there are to display.

❼ When an item is tapped by the user, display a toast notification with the title of that item.

That's everything needed for the first phase of this application. Running the application in the emulator should look like Figure 6-2. Tapping on the marker will display a short toast notification containing the text "New York City." When running the app, remember to target an emulator image that has the Google APIs installed, or else you will receive an error during installation.

Windows Phone

Create a new Windows Phone application project named `Chapter6.WindowsPhoneApp` and add a references to `Microsoft.Phone.Controls.Maps` and `System.Device` to enable

Figure 6-2. Map application for Android

the Windows Phone mapping APIs. Next, open *MainPage.xaml* to start editing the markup for the view. To create a map for this page, you'll need to add a `Map` element, which is found in the `Microsoft.Phone.Controls.Maps` namespace (see Example 6-7). Through the `ZoomBarVisibility` property, we can specify that the map should use the built-in zooming functionality that comes with the control.

 Just as Google does with Google Maps, Microsoft also requires that you obtain an API key in order to utilize Bing Maps in your applications. Information on how to get a Bing Maps API key is available at *https://www.bingmapsportal.com*.

Example 6-7. MainPage.xaml

```
<phone:PhoneApplicationPage
    x:Class="Chapter6.WindowsPhoneApp.MainPage"
    xmlns="http://schemas.microsoft.com/winfx/2006/xaml/presentation"
    xmlns:x="http://schemas.microsoft.com/winfx/2006/xaml"
    xmlns:phone="clr-namespace:Microsoft.Phone.Controls;assembly=Microsoft.Phone"
    xmlns:shell="clr-namespace:Microsoft.Phone.Shell;assembly=Microsoft.Phone"
    xmlns:d="http://schemas.microsoft.com/expression/blend/2008"
    xmlns:mc="http://schemas.openxmlformats.org/markup-compatibility/2006"
    mc:Ignorable="d" FontFamily="{StaticResource PhoneFontFamilyNormal}"
    FontSize="{StaticResource PhoneFontSizeNormal}"
    Foreground="{StaticResource PhoneForegroundBrush}"
```

```
    SupportedOrientations="Portrait" Orientation="Portrait"
    shell:SystemTray.IsVisible="True"
    xmlns:my="clr-
namespace:Microsoft.Phone.Controls.Maps;assembly=Microsoft.Phone.Controls.Maps"
    d:DesignHeight="768" d:DesignWidth="480">

    <Grid x:Name="LayoutRoot" Background="Transparent">
        <Grid.RowDefinitions>
            <RowDefinition Height="Auto"/>
            <RowDefinition Height="*"/>
        </Grid.RowDefinitions>

        <StackPanel x:Name="TitlePanel" Grid.Row="0" Margin="12,17,0,28">
            <TextBlock x:Name="ApplicationTitle" Text="Chapter 6" Style="{StaticResource
PhoneTextNormalStyle}"/>
            <TextBlock x:Name="PageTitle" Text="map" Margin="9,-7,0,0"
Style="{StaticResource PhoneTextTitle1Style}"/>
        </StackPanel>

        <Grid x:Name="ContentPanel" Grid.Row="1" Margin="12,0,12,0">
            <my:Map Name="Map" Height="600" Width="450"
                    ZoomBarVisibility="Visible"
                    CredentialsProvider="Your Key Goes Here" />
        </Grid>
    </Grid>
</phone:PhoneApplicationPage>
```

Next, open *MainPage.xaml.cs* to edit the page's code-behind file:

Example 6-8. MainPage.xaml.cs

```
using System.Device.Location;
using System.Windows;
using System.Windows.Navigation;
using Microsoft.Phone.Controls;
using Microsoft.Phone.Controls.Maps;

namespace Chapter6.WindowsPhoneApp
{
    public partial class MainPage : PhoneApplicationPage
    {
        public MainPage()
        {
            InitializeComponent();
        }

        protected override void OnNavigatedTo(NavigationEventArgs e)
        {
            base.OnNavigatedTo(e);

            var newYorkCity = new GeoCoordinate(40.716667, -74);  ❶
            Map.SetView(newYorkCity, 13);  ❷

            var pin = new Pushpin();  ❸
            pin.Location = newYorkCity;  ❹
```

```
            pin.Content = "New York City"; ❺

            Map.Children.Add(pin); ❻
        }
    }
}
```

❶ Create a GeoCoordinate object to represent New York City's location.

❷ Set the view of the map to be centered at that location, with an initial zoom level of 13.

❸ Create a new Pushpin object, that will represent a marker on the map.

❹ Set the pin's location to be New York City's coordinates.

❺ Attach a label to the pin that says "New York City."

❻ Add this pin to the map.

That's all you need for the first phase of this application. If you run the app now in the emulator, it should look like Figure 6-3.

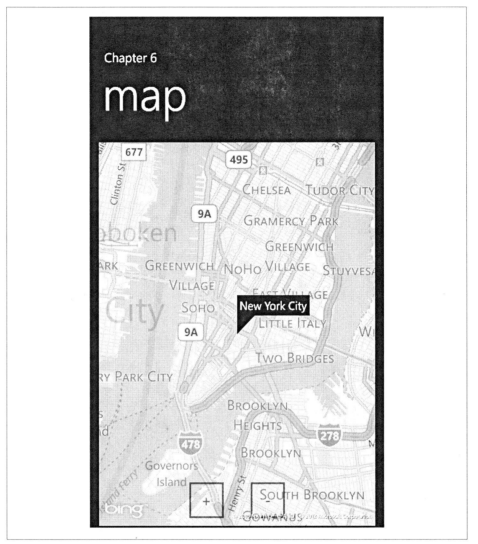

Figure 6-3. Map application for Windows Phone

Mocking Location

When trying to test out a location-based application, it certainly wouldn't be ideal if you had to travel around the world just to see how it responds to different locations. Fortunately, each platform provides its own way of allowing you to send in fake location data to the emulator. You can make it think it's anywhere you want it to be. Before diving into the different location APIs, let's take a quick look at how to mock out your location in each of the emulators. Table 6-1 shows some example locations around the world that you can use while testing, but feel free to substitute any location you like.

Table 6-1. Sample location data

City	Latitude	Longitude
Berlin	52.516667	13.416667
London	51.5	0.133333
New York City	40.716667	−74
Rio de Janeiro	−22.9	−43.233333
Sydney	−33.866667	151.216667

iOS

In the iOS simulator, you can access the location tools by opening the Debug→Location menu. In there, you'll find different options for setting the simulator's location, including Apple's headquarters in Cupertino, which is also the simulator's default location. If you select the Custom Location option, you will be presented with a dialog where you can enter the latitude and longitude of where you would like to go (see Figure 6-4).

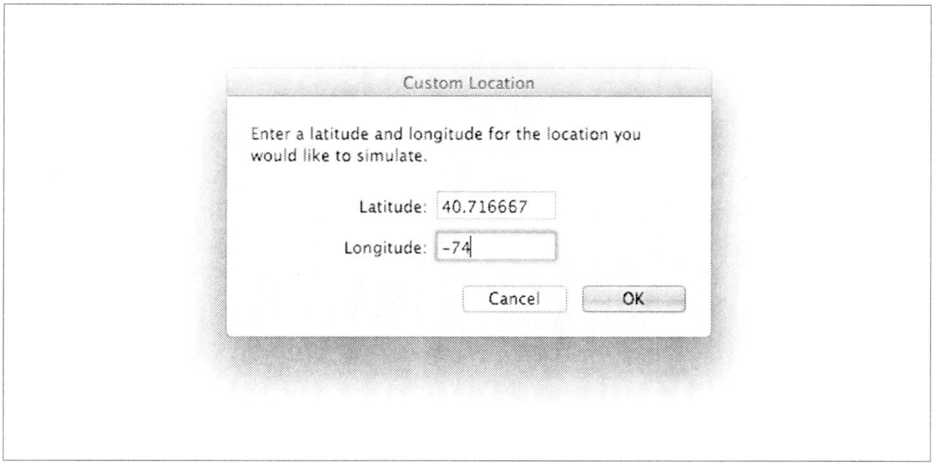

Figure 6-4. Setting a custom location in the iOS simulator

Android

There are several options for sending mock location data to the Android emulator, but the easiest way is to use the *Dalvik Debug Monitor Server (DDMS)*, a tool that comes with the Android SDK. If you navigate to the folder in which you installed the Android SDK, you can find DDMS inside the tools subfolder. This is a very powerful tool that can do much more than send fake location data, so it's worth taking some time to explore it. Through DDMS you can access the device logs and memory information, as well as take screenshots and much more.

After you launch the application select the emulator in the panel on the left, and then navigate to the Emulator Control tab on the right. In this tab you'll find the Location Controls where you can send locations to the emulator (see Figure 6-5).

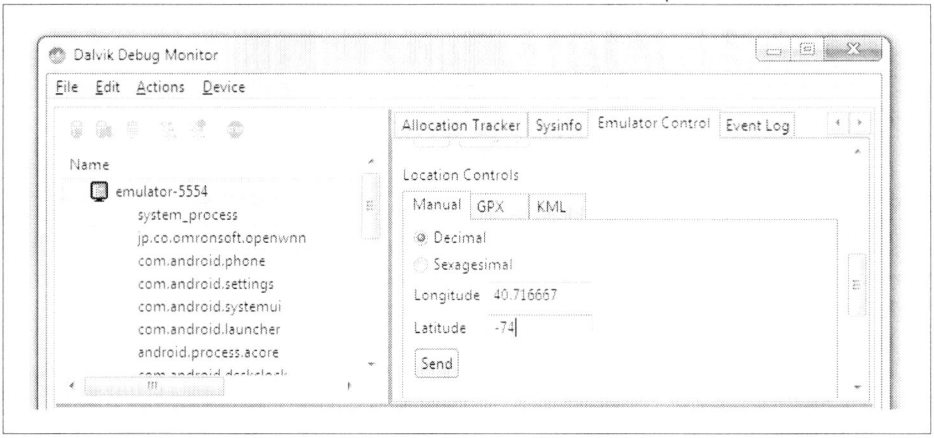

Figure 6-5. Setting a custom location using DDMS

Windows Phone

Starting with version 7.1, the Windows Phone SDK includes a built-in location simulator. To activate the location simulator, start by moving your mouse cursor towards the upper right corner of the emulator. This will reveal a toolbar with various options, such as changing the device orientation or setting the size of the emulator. At the bottom of this toolbar is a chevron icon. Click on this icon to expose the Additional Tools panel, which contains tools for simulating device features like the accelerometer and location sensors.

In the Location tab of this panel, you will find a map that you can zoom and pan around. Clicking on the map will add a pin to that point. By toggling the Live button at the top, you can choose whether to record a series of movements that you can play back later in sequence, or whether each new pin will change the emulator's location immediately (see Figure 6-6). For the purposes of this chapter, you can leave it set to the live mode.

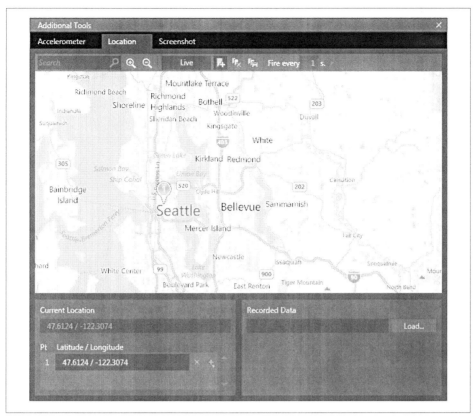

Figure 6-6. Setting a custom location in the Windows Phone emulator

Using Location Data

All three platforms expose robust APIs that allow you to easily tap into the user's current location within your applications. Despite the fact that all three of these APIs are independent of one another, there are many things they have in common, both in how they obtain the data and best practices for how to approach designing your application.

There are three sensors available for devices to determine the current location:

1. Cellular signal
2. Wi-Fi connection
3. GPS signal

These sensors are listed in increasing order of accuracy, so GPS provides the finest level of precision and cellular signal the coarsest. Naturally, this has implications for how you should approach building your apps in order to provide the best possible user experience.

Accuracy

As is often the case, with great power comes great impact on battery life. When designing a location-aware application, you should think about the level of accuracy you need in the user's location. Obtaining finer location information requires using more accurate sensors, which in turn consumes more power. For example, if you were building a weather application you might only care about the region a user was in rather than the street she is standing on. As such, there is no need to fire up the expensive GPS sensor when a cheaper one will suffice.

Frequency

Along the same lines, another thing to keep in mind is how often you need location updates. You can think of this frequency not just in terms of a polling time interval but also how far the user must move before you need an updated location. Depending on the platform, you will be able to specify preferences for one or both of these criteria. Does your app need to know when the user moves one meter from his last position, or can it wait until he moves fifty? Fine tuning the frequency of location updates can go a long way in preserving battery life, and helping the overall performance of your application. Taking that even further, it's a good practice to unsubscribe from location updates if you no longer need them.

Availability

Applications should also be careful to handle gracefully when there is no location data available at a given time. If your app absolutely depends on location data, you should at least display a message to the user indicating the situation, but ideally the app will simply degrade gracefully with regard to the user's location, remaining functional until the data becomes available. Even when the data is available, it can still take some time before it is delivered to your application. For example, if the GPS on a device is not already active, it can take a little while to start up and obtain its first reading. Be careful to handle these situations properly within your applications in order to deliver the best possible solution to the user.

iOS

With those guidelines in mind, let's dig a little deeper into Core Location, the iOS location framework. The primary class you'll work with when processing location is `CLLocationManager`, which allows you to specify criteria for the kind of data you want and publishes events when the location changes.

To specify the update frequency, `CLLocationManager` exposes the `DistanceFilter` property. This value of this property represents the distance in meters that the user must travel before a location update event is fired. Similarly, the `DesiredAccuracy` property allows you to declare how accurate you want the location to be. iOS will use this value to determine which sensors to use. There are several predefined values you can set this to, found on the CLLocation class:

AccuracyBestForNavigation
: Highest possible accuracy combined with data from other sensors

AccuracyBest
: Highest possible accuracy

AccuracyNearestTenMeters
: Accurate within ten meters

AccuracyHundredMeters
: Accurate within one hundred meters

AccuracyKilometers
: Accurate within one kilometer

AccuracyThreeKilometers
: Accurate within three kilometers

With these in mind, we can now add some location awareness to the app built in the last section. Open *MapViewController.cs*, modifying it according to Example 6-9:

Example 6-9. MapViewController.cs (updates only)

```
using MonoTouch.CoreLocation;
using MonoTouch.MapKit;
using MonoTouch.UIKit;

namespace Chapter6.MonoTouchApp
{
    public partial class MapViewController : UIViewController
    {
        private CLLocationManager _locationManager;

        // ...existing code in class...

        public override void ViewDidLoad()
        {
            // ...existing code in method...

            _locationManager = new CLLocationManager(); ❶
            _locationManager.UpdatedLocation += locationUpdated; ❷
            _locationManager.DistanceFilter = 20; ❸
            _locationManager.DesiredAccuracy = CLLocation.AccuracyHundredMeters; ❹

            _locationManager.StartUpdatingLocation(); ❺
        }

        public override void ViewDidUnload()
        {
            base.ViewDidUnload ();

            _locationManager.StopUpdatingLocation(); ❻
```

```
        }

        private void locationUpdated (object sender, CLLocationUpdatedEventArgs e)
        {
            Map.CenterCoordinate = e.NewLocation.Coordinate; ❼
            Map.Region = MKCoordinateRegion.FromDistance (e.NewLocation.Coordinate, 5000,
5000);

            var annotation = new MapAnnotation("Current Location", e.NewLocation.Coordinate);
            Map.AddAnnotation(annotation); ❽
        }
    }
}
```

❶ Create a new instance of `CLLocationManager` to use for gathering location data.

❷ Assign an event handler for when location updates are published.

❸ Specify that the application only needs to be notified when the user has moved at least 20 meters since the last event.

❹ Specify that the application needs a location that is accurate within 100 meters.

❺ Start listening for location updates.

❻ When the user navigates away from this screen, stop listening for location updates to help preserve battery power.

❼ When the location is updated, re-center the map on the new location.

❽ Create a marker at the new location, labeled as "Current Location."

If you run the application again, you should see that the map is now centered at Cupertino, which is the emulator's default location. Updating the location manually as described earlier in the chapter will cause the map to update to the new location, placing a marker there. Previously placed markers are left on the map, so you can still see them even after sending in new locations.

 You can use the pinch-to-zoom gesture in the simulator in order to zoom in and out on the map. While your mouse cursor is over the screen, hold down the option key on the keyboard, which will expose two circles over the screen, representing finger placement. With these exposed, you can click and drag over the screen to simulate the gesture.

Android

In order to gain access to location data in Android applications, you must request the appropriate permissions. These permissions will be shown to the user when they install your application, so that they know exactly what your app will be doing. The two main permissions you can request for location data are:

ACCESS_COARSE_LOCATION
Allows access to location data from cellular and Wi-Fi signals

ACCESS_FINE_LOCATION
Allows access to location data from the GPS

You can specify the permissions required by your application under the Android Manifest tab of the project's properties dialog (see Figure 6-7. For the purposes of this application, you can just select them both.

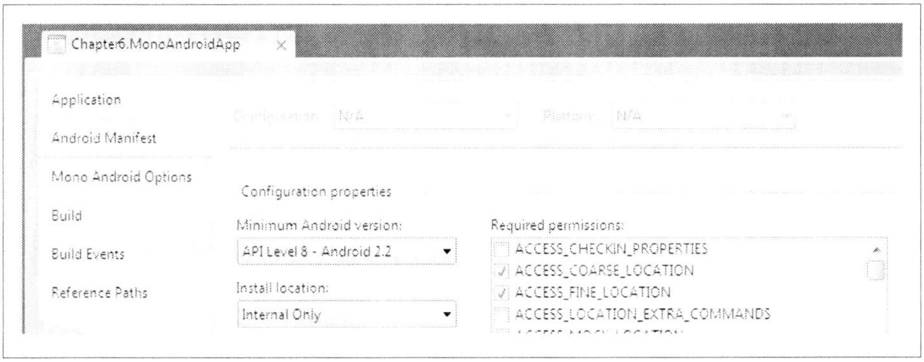

Figure 6-7. Requesting permissions for location data

In order to tell Android how to determine which location provider to use, you can build up a `Criteria` object, which includes several properties that you can customize. The first property is `Accuracy`, which can be set to:

- `NoRequirement`
- `Fine`
- `Coarse`

These values can be found in the `Accuracy` enumeration. As the names imply, `Fine` and `Coarse` correspond to the two permissions mentioned earlier. Android also allows you to request a maximum power level to be used in gathering the location data through the `PowerRequirement` property, and can be set to values from the `Power` enumeration:

- `NoRequirement`
- `High`
- `Medium`
- `Low`

In the event that no provider is available that meets the given criteria, Android will loosen the criteria until it finds one. To define a class that can respond to location updates, it must implement the `ILocationListener` interface, which includes methods of handling when there are changes in location and availability. To simplify things for this example, simply extend LocationActivity to implement the interface (see Example 6-10). This is not a requirement and can be implemented as a separate class as well.

Example 6-10. LocationActivity.cs (updates only)

```
using Android.App;
using Android.GoogleMaps;
using Android.Locations;
using Android.OS;
using Android.Widget;

namespace Chapter6.MonoAndroidApp
{
    [Activity(Label = "Map", MainLauncher = true, Icon = "@drawable/icon")]
    public class LocationActivity : MapActivity ,ILocationListener
    {
        // ...existing code in class...

        private LocationManager _locationManager;

        protected override void OnCreate(Bundle bundle)
        {
            // ...existing code in method...

            _locationManager = (LocationManager)GetSystemService(LocationService); ❶
        }

        protected override void OnResume()
        {
            base.OnResume();

            var criteria = new Criteria(); ❷
            criteria.PowerRequirement = Power.NoRequirement;
            criteria.Accuracy = Accuracy.Coarse;

            string bestProvider = _locationManager.GetBestProvider(criteria, true); ❸

            _locationManager.RequestLocationUpdates(bestProvider, 5000, 20, this); ❹
        }

        protected override void OnPause()
        {
            base.OnPause();

            _locationManager.RemoveUpdates(this); ❺
        }

        public void OnLocationChanged(Location location) ❻
        {
            var currentLocation = new GeoPoint((int)(location.Latitude * 1e6), (int)
(location.Longitude * 1e6));

            _mapOverlay.Add(currentLocation, "Current Location");

            _map.Controller.AnimateTo(currentLocation);
```

```
        }

        public void OnProviderDisabled(string provider)
        {
            // called when a provider is disabled
        }

        public void OnProviderEnabled(string provider)
        {
            // called when a provider is enabled
        }

        public void OnStatusChanged(string provider, Availability status, Bundle extras) ❼
        {
            Toast
                .MakeText(this, "Status for " + provider + " changed to " + status,
ToastLength.Short)
                .Show();
        }
    }
}
```

❶ Store a reference to the system's location service.

❷ Create a `Criteria` saying that there is no power requirement and only coarse location data is needed. This is called from `OnResume()` so that it will be called again if the user navigates back to the activity.

❸ Find the best provider given the criteria.

❹ Request location updates, specifying a minimum of five seconds and 20 meters in between updates.

❺ When navigating away from this activity, stop listening for location updates.

❻ The `OnLocationChanged()` method is called whenever there is an updated location. Re-center the map on the new location and add a new marker.

❼ `OnStatusChanged()` is called when the availability of location data is changed. When this changes, print a toast message with the new status.

You may have noticed that you didn't create your own instance of `LocationManager`. Android maintains a set of system-level services designed to manage things like location information, WiFi connectivity, and downloads. These services are shared across the system, and can be accessed by calling `GetSystemService()` with the appropriate name, which in this case is found in a `const string` named `LocationService`.

If you run the application again in the emulator, it should behave similarly to the iOS version. Sending in new locations through DDMS will cause the map to move to that location, adding a new marker.

Windows Phone

The main class in the Windows Phone location API that you interact with is GeoCoordinateWatcher. As seen in APIs on the other platforms, you can specify a minimum distance that must be traveled in order for a new location update to be published by setting the MovementThreshold property, which is measured in meters. You can also configure the desired accuracy by sending in a value from the GeoPositionAccuracy enumeration into the constructor. Possible values are:

High
> Obtain the most accurate location data available, most likely from the GPS

Default
> Optimize location data accuracy based on performance and power consumption

As you'll see in this example, there are also events exposed by GeoCoordinateWatcher that allow you to handle when there are updates to location or the availability of location data. Open *MainPage.xaml.cs* and modify it to look like Example 6-11.

Example 6-11. MainPage.xaml.cs (updates only)

```
using System.Device.Location;
using System.Windows;
using System.Windows.Navigation;
using Microsoft.Phone.Controls;
using Microsoft.Phone.Controls.Maps;

namespace Chapter6.WindowsPhoneApp
{
    public partial class MainPage : PhoneApplicationPage
    {
        // ...existing code in class...

        private GeoCoordinateWatcher _locationWatcher;

        protected override void OnNavigatedTo(NavigationEventArgs e)
        {
            // ...existing code in method...

            _locationWatcher = new GeoCoordinateWatcher(GeoPositionAccuracy.Default); ❶
            _locationWatcher.MovementThreshold = 20;
            _locationWatcher.PositionChanged += positionChanged; ❷
            _locationWatcher.StatusChanged += statusChanged; ❸
            _locationWatcher.Start(); ❹
        }

        protected override void OnNavigatedFrom(NavigationEventArgs e)
        {
            base.OnNavigatedFrom(e);

            _locationWatcher.Stop(); ❺
        }
```

```
        private void statusChanged(object sender, GeoPositionStatusChangedEventArgs e)
        {
            MessageBox.Show("Status changed to: " + e.Status); ❻
        }

        private void positionChanged(object sender,
GeoPositionChangedEventArgs<GeoCoordinate> e) ❼
        {
            var newPositionPin = new Pushpin();
            newPositionPin.Location = e.Position.Location;
            newPositionPin.Content = "Current Location";

            Map.Children.Add(newPositionPin);

            Map.SetView(e.Position.Location, 7);
        }
    }
}
```

❶ Create a new GeoCoordinateWatcher instance, using the default accuracy level and a minimum threshold of 20 meters between updates.

❷ Assign an event handler for when location updates are published.

❸ Assign an event handler for when location data availability changes.

❹ Start listening for location updates.

❺ When navigating away from this page, stop listening for location updates.

❻ When there is a status change, display a message with the new status.

❼ When the location changes, re-center the map and add a new marker to the new location.

Running the application in the emulator now should behave just like the other two platforms. You can send in new locations using the emulator tools described earlier in the chapter to add new markers and re-center the map.

Summary

In this chapter, we explored the geolocation frameworks exposed by each platform. The sample application demonstrated how to display an interactive map to the user, place markers on the map, and tie it together with the user's location to provide a personalized experience. We also covered how to provide mock location data to the emulators in order to test out location changes. In exploring these frameworks, we also saw that even though each provides its own distinct implementations, there are many overlapping aspects among them, ranging from battery life impact to performance optimizations. Location awareness is a powerful way to create a very compelling user experience in your applications, allowing them to interact more profoundly with the world around them.

Creating Android Virtual Devices

Because there are so many variations of Android devices out there, Android allows you to customize many different aspects of an emulator image, such as the screen size, the version of the operating system, the amount of memory, and much more. This allows you to test out how your application will behave under these different conditions without having to own every Android device on the market. The installer provided by Xamarin will create several emulator images for you with different operating system versions in order to allow you to get started more quickly. This section will walk you through how to create new virtual devices of your own, allowing you to configure them however you'd like.

 The Android emulator differs from other platforms in that it is a full emulator, rather than a simulator. What this means is that it is emulating the full ARM instruction set in software, resulting in an experience that can sometimes be painfully slow. When running your applications in the emulator, just remember that poor performance is often due to the emulator itself rather than Mono for Android.

Start out by opening up Android's *SDK Manager*, which is located in the root folder of the Android SDK on your computer. This application allows you to choose which SDKs you want to install. Typically, the simplest route is to just let it install everything, but you can also pick and choose which packages you care to install if you wish. When new Android SDKs are released they will show up in this application for you to download and install.

Once you download the SDK for a particular version of Android, you will be able to create virtual devices for that version. Listed under each version's section in SDK Manager, you'll find packages for the standard SDK platform, samples, and the Google APIs (see Figure A-1). For some versions, you may also find other packages available for you to use, such as customized versions of Android developed by different Android vendors like Motorola Mobility and HTC, or other supplementary APIs made available by Google.

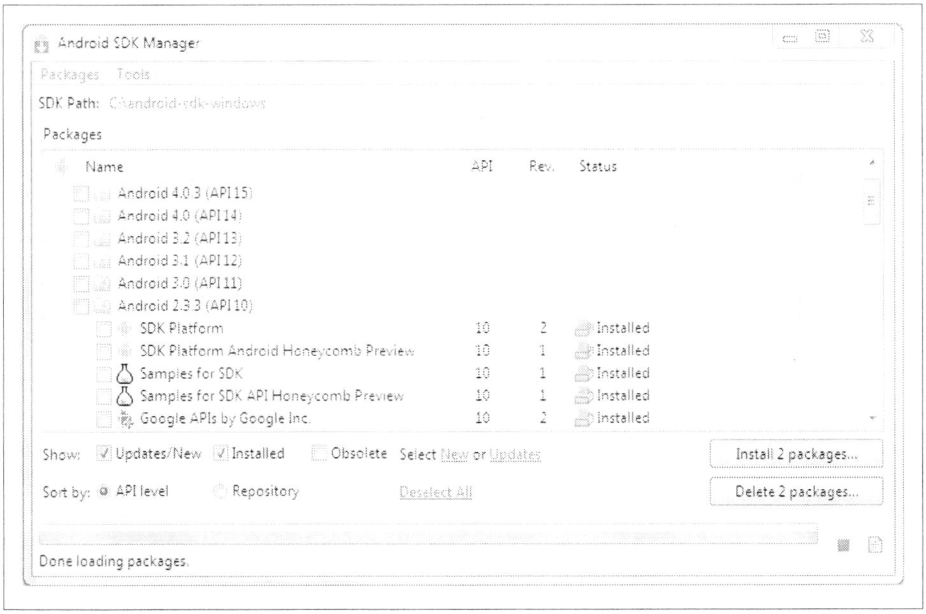

Figure A-1. Android SDK Manager

As described in Chapter 6, even though Google Maps is available for you to use on most Android devices, it is technically not part of the stock Android installation. In order to use these APIs in an emulator image, you will need to create that image using the Google API package for the Android version you want. You can refer back to Chapter 6 for more details on the reasons behind this requirement.

To demonstrate creating a new virtual device, we will set up a Gingerbread device using API level, which includes the Google APIs. As such, make sure you have installed that SDK package on your computer (see Figure A-1). Next, open *AVD (Android Virtual Device) Manager*, which is located in the same folder as SDK Manager. This tool allows you to configure different virtual devices using any configuration you want.

When you launch AVD Manager, you will first see a list of existing virtual devices that are available to you. From here, you can start any of these devices, modify them, or create new ones. On the right side of the AVD Manager window, click on New to start creating a new device. Configure the device to have the following:

- **Name**: GingerbreadMaps
- **Target**: Google APIs (Google Inc.) – API Level 10
- **SD Card Size**: 512 MB
- **Skin**: Built-in QVGA

Once you set it up, your window should look similar to Figure A-2. The reason for choosing QVGA here for the screen resolution is to try to improve performance by

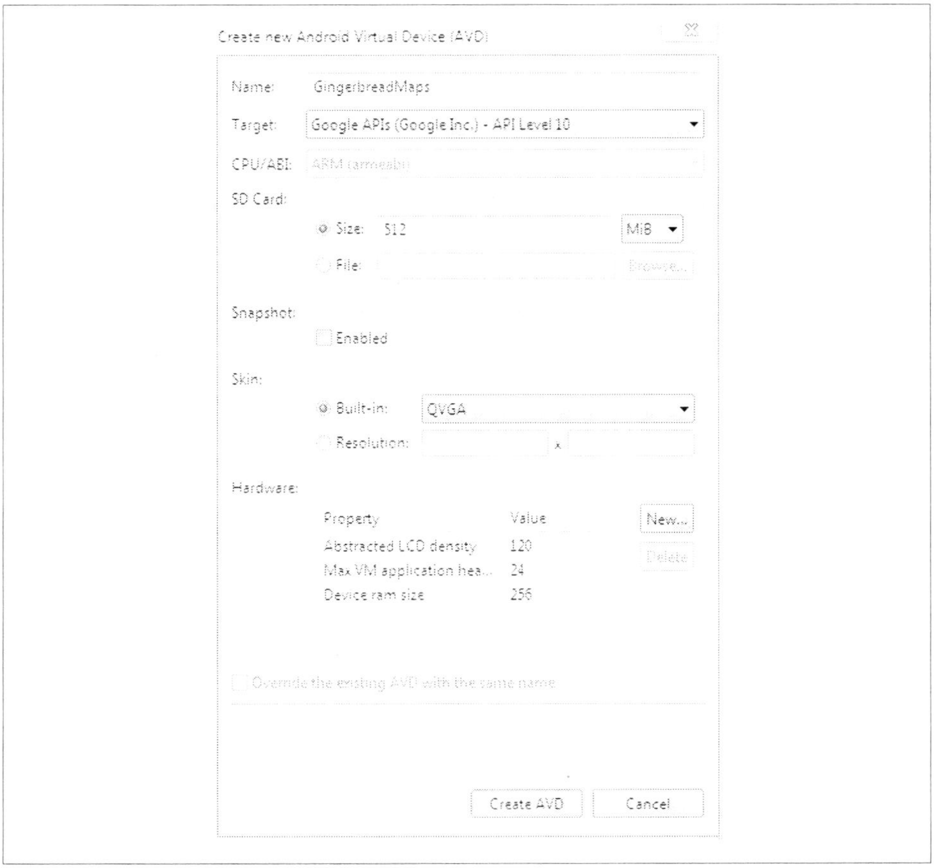

Figure A-2. Creating a new virtual device

keeping the screen resolution down. A smaller screen size means that the emulator needs to do less work to draw the screen, which can go a long way in making the emulator much more usable. Click on the Create AVD button to save the device and make it available for testing your applications.

> Even though you can start a virtual device from inside AVD Manager, it is generally not recommended when developing with Mono for Android. By default, Android will start up the emulator with a partition size that is often too small for the Mono for Android development platform, so you may run into issues with running out of space. Instead, you should start the emulator from inside of Visual Studio or MonoDevelop, as described in Chapter 2, which will result in the emulator starting up with a larger partition size and avoid these problems.

Further Reading

This book aims to get your feet wet with iOS, Android, and Windows Phone, but there is plenty more to explore for all of them. This section will provide some starting points for digging deeper into each of the platforms on its own. One thing to keep in mind for MonoTouch and Mono for Android is that resources written with the native languages in mind, Objective-C and Java, are still very useful even though you're working in C# since the Mono products provide bindings to the native APIs. You're still writing native applications so many of the same concepts and classes apply, regardless of the language.

iOS

Books

Professional iPhone Programming with MonoTouch and .NET/C#

Wallace B. McClure, Rory Blyth, Craig Dunn, Chris Hardy, Martin Bowling

Wrox, 2010

http://www.wrox.com/WileyCDA/WroxTitle/Professional-iPhone-Programming-with -MonoTouch-and-NET-C-.productCd-047063782X.html

Learning MonoTouch: A Hands-On Guide to Building iOS Applications with C# and .NET

Michael Bluestein

Addison-Wesley Professional, 2011

http://www.informit.com/store/product.aspx?isbn=0321719921

Developing C# Apps for iPhone and iPad using MonoTouch: iOS Apps Development for .NET Developers

Bryan Costanich

Apress, 2011

http://www.apress.com/9781430231745

Web

Xamarin: MonoTouch Documentation

http://docs.xamarin.com/ios

Xamarin: Sample Applications and Code

http://new-docs.xamarin.com/Samples/MonoTouch

Apple: iOS Dev Center

https://developer.apple.com/devcenter/ios

Android

Books

Professional Android Programming with Mono for Android and .NET/C#

Wallace B. McClure, Nathan Blevins, John J. Croft, IV, Jonathan Dick, Chris Hardy

Wrox, 2012

http://www.wrox.com/WileyCDA/WroxTitle/Professional-Android-Programming-with -Mono-for-Android-and-NET-C-.productCd-1118026438.html

Programming Android

Zigurd Mednieks, Laird Dornin, G. Blake Meike, Masumi Nakamura

O'Reilly Media, 2011

http://shop.oreilly.com/product/0636920010364.do

Web

Xamarin: Mono for Android Documentation

http://docs.xamarin.com/android

Xamarin: Sample Applications and Code

http://new-docs.xamarin.com/Samples/MonoForAndroid

Google: Android Documentation

http://developer.android.com

Windows Phone

Books

Programming Windows Phone 7

Microsoft, 2010

Charles Petzold

http://www.amazon.com/Microsoft-Silverlight-Edition-Programming-Windows/dp/0735656673

Migrating to Windows Phone

Jesse Liberty, Jeff Blankenburg

Apress, 2011

http://www.apress.com/mobile/windows-phone/9781430238164

101 Windows Phone 7 Apps

Sams, 2011

Adam Nathan

http://www.informit.com/store/product.aspx?isbn=0672335522

Web

31 Days of Mango

http://31daysofmango.com

Jeff Blankenburg's Blog

http://jeffblankenburg.com

Jesse Liberty's Blog

http://jesseliberty.com

Windows Phone Developer Training Kit

http://wpdev.ms/wpdevtrain

About the Author

Greg Shackles is a senior software engineer at OLO Online Ordering, based in New York City. An active member of the community, Greg speaks regularly at many user groups and regional events. Greg received both bachelor's and master's degrees in computer science from Stony Brook University. In addition to his passion for technology, he is also an avid fan of heavy metal, baseball, and craft beer, sometimes in combination. His blog, which focuses mainly on .NET and related topics, can be found at *http://www.gregshackles.com*.

Have it your way.

Get even more for your money.

Join the O'Reilly Community, and register the O'Reilly books you own. It's free, and you'll get:

* $4.99 ebook upgrade offer
* 40% upgrade offer on O'Reilly print books
* Membership discounts on books and events
* Free lifetime updates to ebooks and videos
* Multiple ebook formats, DRM FREE
* Participation in the O'Reilly community
* Newsletters
* Account management
* 100% Satisfaction Guarantee

Signing up is easy:

1. **Go to: oreilly.com/go/register**
2. **Create an O'Reilly login.**
3. **Provide your address.**
4. **Register your books.**

Note: English-language books only

To order books online:
oreilly.com/store

For questions about products or an order:
orders@oreilly.com

To sign up to get topic-specific email announcements and/or news about upcoming books, conferences, special offers, and new technologies:
elists@oreilly.com

For technical questions about book content:
booktech@oreilly.com

To submit new book proposals to our editors:
proposals@oreilly.com

O'Reilly books are available in multiple DRM-free ebook formats. For more information:
oreilly.com/ebooks

O'REILLY®

Spreading the knowledge of innovators   oreilly.com